The Monograph

The volumes within the *Tall Buildings and Urban Environment* series correspond to the Council's group and committee structure. The present listing includes all current topical committees. Some are collaborating to produce volumes together, and Groups DM and BSS plan, with only a few exceptions, to combine all topics into one volume.

PLANNING AND ENVIRONMENTAL CRITERIA (PC)
Philosophy of Tall Buildings
History of Tall Buildings
Architecture
Rehabilitation, Renovation, Repair
Urban Planning and Design
External Transportation
Parking
Social Effects of the Environment
Socio-Political Influences
Design for the Disabled and Elderly
Interior Design
Landscape Architecture

DEVELOPMENT AND MANAGEMENT (DM)
Economics
Ownership and Maintenance
Project Management
Tall Buildings in Developing Countries
Decision-Making Parameters
Development and Investment
Legal Aspects

SYSTEMS AND CONCEPTS (SC)
Cladding
Partitions, Walls, and Ceilings
Structural Systems
Foundation Design
Construction Systems
High-Rise Housing
Prefabricated Tall Buildings
Tall Buildings Using Local Technology
Robots and Tall Buildings
Application of Systems Methodology

BUILDING SERVICE SYSTEMS (BSS)
HVAC/Energy Conservation
Plumbing and Fire Protection
Electrical Systems

CRITERIA AND LOADING (CL)
Gravity Loads and Temperature Effects
Earthquake Loading and Response
Wind Loading and Wind Effects
Fire
Accidental Loading
Safety and Quality Assurance
Motion Perception and Tolerance

TALL STEEL BUILDINGS (SB)
Commentary on Structural Standards
Methods of Analysis and Design
Stability
Design Methods Based on Stiffness
Fatigue Assessment & Ductility Assurance
Connections
Cold-Formed Steel
Load and Resistance Factor Design (Limits States Design)
Mixed Construction

TALL CONCRETE AND MASONRY BUILDINGS (CB)
Commentary on Structural Standards
Selection of Structural Systems
Optimization
Elastic Analysis
Nonlinear Analysis and Limit Design
Stability
Stiffness and Crack Control
Precast Panel Structures
Creep, Shrinkage, & Temperature Effects
Cast-in-Place Concrete
Precast-Prestressed Concrete
Masonry Structures

High-Tech Buildings
Vertical & Horizontal Transportation
Environmental Design
Urban Services

The basic objective of the Council's Monograph is to document the most recent developments to the state of the art in the field of tall buildings and their role in the urban habitat. The following volumes can be ordered through the Council.

Planning and Design of Tall Buildings, 5 volumes (1978-1981 by ASCE)

Developments in Tall Buildings–1983 (Van Nostrand Reinhold Company)

Advances in Tall Buildings (1986, Van Nostrand Reinhold Company)

High-Rise Buildings: Recent Progress (1986, Council on Tall Buildings)

Second Century of the Skyscraper (1988 Van Nostrand Reinhold Company)

Tall Buildings: 2000 and Beyond, 2 volumes (1990 & 1991, Council on Tall Buildings)

Council Headquarters
Lehigh University, Building 13
Bethlehem, Pennsylvania 18015 USA

Cladding

Library of Congress Cataloging-in-Publication Data

Cladding / Council on Tall Buildings and Urban Habitat, Committee 12A ; contributors,
    Bruce Bassler...[et al.] ; editorial group, Marcy Li Wang, chairman ;
    I. Sakamoto, vice-chairman ; Bruce L. Bassler, editor ; contributors,
        p.   cm. — (Tall building systems and concepts) (Tall buildings and urban
    environment series) (Monograph)
    Includes bibliographical references (p.   ) and indexes.
    ISBN 0-07-012534-1
    1. Curtain walls—Design and construction.   2. Tall buildings—Design and
construction.   I. Wang, Marcy Li.   II. Sakamoto, I. (Isao)   III. Bassler, Bruce L.
IV. Council on Tall Buildings and Urban Habitat. Committee
12A   V. Series.   VI. Series: Tall buildings and urban environment
series.   VII. Series: Monograph (Council on Tall Buildings and Urban Habitat)
    TH2238.C53   1992   92-5047
    698—dc20   CIP

1 2 3 4 5 6 7 8 9 0   DOC/DOC   9 8 7 6 5 4 3 2

ISBN   0-07-012534-1

*For the Council on Tall Buildings and Urban Habitat, Lynn S. Beedle is
the Editor-in-Chief and Dolores B. Rice is the Managing Editor.*

*For McGraw-Hill, the sponsoring editor for this book was Joel Stein, the
editing supervisor was Peggy Lamb, and the production supervisor was
Pamela A. Pelton. This book was set in Times Roman by McGraw-Hill's
Professional Book Group composition unit.*

Printed and bound by R. R. Donnelley & Sons Company.

Council on Tall Buildings and Urban Habitat

Steering Group

Council on Tall Buildings and Urban Habitat

Contributors

Boundary Layer Wind Tunnel Laboratory (U. Western Ontario), London
H. K. Cheng & Partners Ltd., Hong Kong
Douglas Specialist Contractors Ltd:, Aldridge
The George Hyman Construction Co., Bethesda
Johnson Fain and Pereira Assoc., Los Angeles
LeMessurier Consultants Inc., Cambridge
W. L. Meinhardt & Partners Pty. Ltd., Melbourne
Obayashi Corporation, Tokyo
PSM International, Chicago
Tooley & Company, Los Angeles
Nabih Youssef and Associates, Los Angeles

Contributing Participants

Adviesbureau Voor Bouwtechniele bv, Arnhem
American Institute of Steel Construction, Chicago
Anglo American Property Services (Pty) Ltd., Johannesburg
Artech, Inc., Taipei
Austin Commercial, Inc., Dallas
Australian Institute of Steel Construction, Milsons Point
B.C.V. Progetti S.r.l., Milano
Bechtel Corporation, San Francisco
W.S. Bellows Construction Corp., Houston
Alfred Benesch & Co., Chicago
BMP Consulting Engineers, Hong Kong
Bornhorst & Ward Pty. Ltd., Spring Hill
Bovis Limited, London
Bramalea Ltd., Dallas
Brandow & Johnston Associates, Los Angeles
Brooke Hillier Parker, Hong Kong
Campeau Corp., Toronto
CBM Engineers, Houston
Cermak Peterka Petersen, Inc., Fort Collins
Connell Wagner (NSW) Pty. Ltd., Sydney
Construction Consulting Laboratory, Dallas
CPP, Inc., Fort Collins
Crane Fulview Door Co., Lake Bluff
Crone & Associates Pty. Ltd., Sydney
Crow Construction Co., New York
Davis Langdon & Everest, London
DeSimone, Chaplin & Dobryn, New York
Dodd Pacific Engineering, Inc., Seattle
Englekirk, Hart, and Sobel, Inc., Los Angeles
Falcon Steel Company, Wilmington
Fujikawa Johnson and Associates, Chicago
Gutteridge Haskins & Davey Pty Ltd., Sydney
T.R. Hamzah & Yeang Sdn Bhd, Selangor
Hayakawa Associates, Los Angeles
Hellmuth, Obata & Kassabaum, Inc., San Francisco
Honeywell, Inc., Minneapolis
INTEMAC, Madrid
International Iron & Steel Institute, Brussels
Johnson & Nielsen, Irvine
Irwin Johnston & Partners, Sydney
KPFF Consulting Engineers, Seattle
Lend Lease Design Group Ltd., Sydney
Stanley D. Lindsey & Assoc., Nashville
Lohan Associates, Inc., Chicago
Martin & Bravo, Inc., Honolulu
Enrique Martinez-Romero, S.A., Mexico
McWilliam Consulting Engineers, Brisbane

Mitchell McFarlane Brentnall & Partners Intl. Ltd., Hong Kong
Mitsubishi Estate Co., Ltd., Tokyo
Moh and Associates, Inc., Taipei
Mueser Rutledge Consulting Engineers, New York
Multiplex Construction (NSW) Pty. Ltd., Sydney
Nihon Sekkei, U.S.A., Ltd., Los Angeles
Nikken Sekkei Ltd., Tokyo
Norman Disney & Young, Brisbane
O'Brien-Kreitzberg & Associates, Inc., Pennsauken
Ove Arup & Partners, Sydney
Pacific Atlas Development Corp., Los Angeles
Peddle Thorp Australia Pty. Ltd., Australia
Peddle, Thorp & Walker Arch., Sydney
Perkins & Will, Chicago
J. Roger Preston & Partners, Hong Kong
Projest SA Empreendimentos e Servicos Technicos, Rio de Janeiro
Rahulan Zain Associates, Kuala Lumpur
Ranhill Bersekkutu Sdn Bhd., Kuala Lumpur
Rankine & Hill, Wellington
RFB Consulting Architects, Johannesburg
Robert Rosenwasser Associates, PC, New York
Emery Roth & Sons Intl, Inc., New York
Rowan Williams Davies & Irwin, Inc., Guelph
Sepakat Setia Perunding (Sdn.) Bhd., Kuala Lumpur
Shimizu Corporation, Tokyo
South African Institute of Steel Construction, Johannesburg
Steel Reinforcement Institute of Australia, Sydney
Steen Consultants Pte. Ltd., Singapore
Stigter Clarey & Partners, Sydney
Studio Finzi, Nova E Castellani, Milano
Taylor Thompson Whitting Pty Ltd., St. Leonards
Pedro Ramirez Vazquez, Arquitecto, Pedregal de San Angel
VIPAC Engineers & Scientists Ltd., Melbourne
Wargon Chapman Partners, Sydney
Weidlinger Associates, New York
Wimberley, Allison, Tong & Goo, Newport Beach
Wong & Ouyang (HK) Ltd., Hong Kong
Woodward-Clyde Consultants, New York
Yapi Merkezi Inc., Istanbul
Zaldastani Associates, Inc., Boston

Other Books in the Tall Buildings and Urban Environment Series

Cladding

Council on Tall Buildings and Urban Habitat
Committee 12A

CONTRIBUTORS

Bruce Bassler
Lawrence D. Carbary
Hal Iyengar
Jerome M. Klosowski
Victor C. Mahler
Dorothy Reed

Isao Sakamoto
Jerry G. Stockbridge
Marcy Li Wang
Tomonari Yashiri
Gary Zwayer

Editorial Group

Marcy Li Wang, Chairman
Isao Sakamoto, Vice-Chairman
Bruce L. Bassler, Editor

McGraw-Hill, Inc.

New York   St. Louis   San Francisco   Auckland   Bogotá
Caracas   Lisbon   London   Madrid   Mexico   Milan
Montreal   New Delhi   Paris   San Juan   São Paulo
Singapore   Sydney   Tokyo   Toronto

AUTHOR ACKNOWLEDGMENT

This Monograph was prepared by Committee 12A (Cladding) of the Council on Tall Buildings and Urban Habitat as part of the *Tall Buildings and Urban Environment Series*.

Special acknowledgment is due those individuals whose contributions and papers formed the initial contribution to the chapters in this volume. These individuals are:

Hal Iyengar, Foreword
Gary Zwayer, Chapter 1
Lawrence D. Carbary, Chapter 2
Jerome M. Klosowski, Chapter 2
Victor C. Mahler, Chapter 3

Marcy Li Wang, Chapter 4
Dorothy Reed, Chapter 4
Jerry G. Stockbridge, Chapter 5
Isao Sakamoto, Chapter 6
Tomonari Yashiri, Chapter 6

CONTRIBUTORS

The following is a complete list of those who have submitted written material for possible use in the Monograph, whether or not that material was used in the final version. The Committee Chairman and Editor were given quite complete latitude. Frequently, length limitations precluded the inclusion of much valuable material. The Bibliography contains all contributions. The contributors are: Bruce Bassler, Lawrence D. Carbary, Hal Iyengar, Jerome M. Klosowski, Victor C. Mahler, Dorothy Reed, Isao Sakamoto, Jerry G. Stockbridge, Marcy Li Wang, Tomonari Yashiri, and Gary Zwayer.

COMMITTEE MEMBERS

Bruce Bassler, Kevin Baumgartner, Richard Behr, Ormond Robert Berry, Phil Bonzon, Howard D. Eberhart, Gunnar Essunger, Fiorello R. Estuar, Michael D. Flynn, Nicholas Forell, Sidney Freedman, Sigmund A. Freeman, Barry Goodno, I. M. Kadri, Stanislaw Kajfasz, Charles Kilper, Anthony B. Klarich, Jerry Klosowski, Wiliam Knox, Peter L. Lee, Victor C. Mahler, H. Matoba, Kiyoo Matsushita, Ray McCann, Joseph E. Minor, Frank Newby, Sergio Elio Pellegrini, Fabio Penteado, Dorothy Reed, Isao Sakamoto, A. A. Sakhnovsky, Reinhold M. Schuster, Roland L. Sharpe, Jerry Stockbridge, Chuck Thiel, Yoshichika Uchida, Frank Van der Woude, Marcy Li Wang, Sam Webb, Richard Welch, Ewart A. Wetherill, and Tomonari Yashiro.

GROUP LEADERS

The committee on Cladding is part of Group SC of the Council, "Systems and Concepts." The leaders are:

Irwin Cantor, Group Chairman
James Forbes, Group Vice-Chairman
Henry J. Cowan, Group Editor

Foreword

This volume is one of a series of Monographs prepared under the aegis of the Council on Tall Buildings and Urban Habitat, a series that is aimed at updating the documentation of the state-of-the-art of the planning, design, construction, and operation of tall buildings and also their interaction with the urban environment of which they are a part.

The original Monographs contained 52 major topics collected in 5 volumes:

Volume PC: *Planning and Environmental Criteria for Tall Buildings*
Volume SC: *Tall Building Systems and Concepts*
Volume CL: *Tall Building Criteria and Loading*
Volume SB: *Structural Design of Tall Steel Buildings*
Volume CB: *Structural Design of Tall Concrete and Masonry Buildings*

Following the publication of a number of updates to these volumes, it was decided by the Steering Group of the Council to develop a new series. It would be based on the original effort but would focus more strongly on the individual topical committees rather than on the groups. This would do two things. It would free the Council committees from restraints as to length. Also it would permit material on a given topic to more quickly reach the public.

This particular Monograph was prepared by the Council's Committee 12A, *Cladding*. Although based on the original chapter in Volume SC, it concentrates on these important issues:

- Cladding systems and materials
- Joints and sealants, especially in the design and selection process
- Wind and seismic effects
- Testing procedures and recommendations

The Monograph Concept

The Monograph series is intended to be of value to those responsible for planning and design practice. It is prepared for those who plan, design, construct, or operate tall buildings, and who need the latest information as a basis for judgment decisions. It includes a summary and condensation of research findings for design use, it provides a major reference source to recent literature and to recently developed design concepts, and it identifies needed research.

A Monograph is not intended to serve as a primer. Its function is to communicate to all knowledgeable persons in the various fields of expertise the state of the art and most advanced knowledge in those fields. Our message has more to

do with setting design policies and general approaches than with detailed applications. It aims to provide adequate information for experienced general practi-
tioners confronted with their first high-rise, as well as opening new vistas to those
who have designed them in the past.

Direct contributions to this Monograph have come from many people in many
countries. Much of the material has been prepared by practicing engineers and
architects, by those in the industry as well as those in the academic sector. The
Council has seen considerable benefit accrue from the mix of professions, and
this is no less true of the Monograph series itself.

The new series of Monographs, *Tall Buildings and the Urban Environment*, is
international in scope and interdisciplinary in treatment. This gives each committee full rein to explore all aspects of their subject as it relates to other nations and
to other fields of interest. This broadened view, it is hoped, will further bring tall
buildings into proper perspective in all disciplines.

Tall Buildings

A tall building is not defined by its height or number of stories. The important
criterion is whether or not the design is influenced by some aspect of "tallness."
It is a building in which "tallness" strongly influences planning, design, construction, and use. It is a building whose height creates different conditions from those
that exist in "common" buildings of a certain region and period.

The Council

The Council is an activity sponsored by engineering, architectural, construction,
and planning professionals throughout the world, an organization that was established to study and report on all aspects of planning, design, construction, and
operation of tall buildings.

The sponsoring societies of the Council are the American Institute of Archi-
tects (AIA), American Society of Civil Engineers (ASCE), American Planning
Association (APA), American Society of Interior Designers (ASID), International
Association for Bridge and Structural Engineering (IABSE), International Union
of Architects (UIA), Japan Structural Consultants Association (JSCA), and the
Urban Land Institute (ULI).

The Council is concerned not only with buildings themselves but also with the
role of tall buildings in the urban environment and their impact thereon. Such a
concern also involves a systematic study of the whole problem of providing adequate space for life and work, considering not only technological factors, but
social and cultural aspects as well. The Council is not an advocate for tall buildings per se; but in those situations in which they are viable, it seeks to encourage
the use of the latest knowledge in their implementation.

Units, Symbols, References, and Other Details

The general guideline was to use SI metric units first, followed by U.S. Customary System units in parentheses, and also "old" metric when necessary. A con-

version table for units is supplied at the end of the volume. A list of symbols also appears at the end of the volume.

The spelling was agreed at the outset to be "American" English.

A condensation of the relevant references and bibliography will be found at the end of each chapter. Full citations are given only in a composite list at the end of the volume.

From the start, the Tall Building Monograph series has been the prime focus of the Council's activity, and it is intended that its periodic revision and the implementation of its ideas and recommendations should be a continuing activity on both national and international levels. Readers who find that a particular topic needs further treatment are invited to bring it to our attention.

Acknowledgment

This work would not have been possible but for the early financial support of the National Science Foundation, which supported the program out of which this Monograph developed. More recently the major financial support has been from the organizational members, identified in earlier pages of this Monograph, as well as from many individual members. Their confidence is appreciated.

Special mention is due Mr. Leslie E. Robertson of Leslie E. Robertson Associates, New York, New York, USA, who provided assistance in reviewing this Monograph. Acknowledgment is next due the headquarters staff at Lehigh University, with whom it has been our pleasure to be associated, namely Jean Polzer, secretary, and Elizabeth Easley, student assistant.

All those who had a role in the authorship of the volume are identified in the acknowledgment page that follows the title page. Especially important are the contributors whose papers formed the essential first drafts—the starting point.

The primary conceptual and editing work was in the hands of the leaders of the Council's Committee 12A, Cladding. The Chairman is Marcy Li Wang of Marcy Li Wang Architects, Berkeley, California, USA. The Vice-Chairman is Isao Sakamoto of the University of Tokyo, Tokyo, Japan. Comprehensive editing was the effort of Bruce Bassler, Iowa State University, Ames, Iowa, USA.

Overall guidance was provided by the Group Leaders Irwin Cantor, of the Office of Irwin G. Cantor, New York, New York, USA; James Forbes, of Scott Willson Irwin Johnston, Milsons Point, NSW, Australia; and Henry Cowan, of the University of Sydney, Sydney, Australia.

Lynn S. Beedle
Editor-in-Chief

Dolores B. Rice
Managing Editor

Lehigh University
Bethlehem, Pennsylvania
1992

Dedication

This Monograph is dedicated to Fazlur Rahman Khan, and the tall buildings he made possible.

Exterior building enclosures, or claddings, especially in high-rise buildings, have undergone an evolutionary change since the turn of the century. Building enclosures are significantly influenced by the styles and esthetics of architecture apart from various technical aspects. As styles have evolved, so have the systems and materials that compose the exterior. Initial styles involved Romanesque or Gothic type facades that were integrated with the structure as an exterior bearing wall or were built in monolithically with the column of the structure. A later style was characterized by emphasis on vertically, with strips of stone cladding on columns and metal spandrels with set-in-windows, as in the Chrysler Building or the Rockefeller Center buildings in New York. The real separation of the exterior enclosure from the structure as a curtain wall that can merely be attached to the structure emerged with the international styles in the 1950s. They were generally characterized by metal and glass compositions. This led to the development of the curtain wall as a total system, including glass, mullions, and claddings, which could then be separately engineered. Technical considerations included the behavior of glass under wind pressure, temperature movement of the wall, structural attachments, and interaction with the basic structure of the building.

The structuralist trend in the 1960s and 1970s led to an evolution of braced tube or equivalent framed tube structures on the facades. The primary proponent of these systems was Dr. Fazlur Rahman Khan, who devised many such systems. Notable examples are the John Hancock Center in Chicago and One Shell Plaza in Houston. The claddings were directly applied to the structure with windows within the structure as in a punched concrete tubular concept.

The current trend in building exteriors involves a variety of compositions, using different types of stone and metal and glass on the building exteriors, which may utilize setbacks, offsets, and balconies for a variety of esthetic effects.

Over the years, the curtain wall or cladding system has emerged from discretized components to a total system incorporating cladding and window systems engineered for environmental forces, weather protection, energy considerations, and a variety of materials involved in the esthetic composition of the facade. Criteria are driven by systematization and industrialization, and therefore represent a highly engineered system. However, the lack of sufficient information on the in-service performance and material properties has resulted in many cladding failures. It is clear that rational design approaches demand an in-depth understanding of the behavioral aspects of the wall system.

This Monograph details the various technical aspects of the window wall and cladding, including a description of systems, components, and materials and design approaches for wind and earthquake forces. This compilation of basic information is a comprehensive introduction to this essential aspect of the tall building.

Hal Iyengar
Skidmore, Owings & Merrill, Chicago

Preface

This Monograph is about that aspect of tall buildings which is the most visible architectural expression to the admiring or critical public—the cladding system. The relationship between a tall building and its enclosure system is particularly significant, because cladding is not only a critical esthetic component, but it serves in conjunction with demanding technical requirements; the environment is harsh, building movement is severe, and replacement and repair costs are exhorbitant.

The purpose of this Monograph is to succinctly present the most recent theory and practice regarding the performance and design of cladding systems to professionals, students, and educators in the building design fields. Like many aspects of building design, common practice in cladding design varies not only from continent to continent, but from region to region within a given country. In its treatment of the topics, the Monograph attempts to reflect the diversity of cladding design in North America, Europe, and Asia. Given the vast array of systems and the pace of technological development, the Monograph serves those who design buildings as well as those who are simply interested in learning more about them.

The support of the Graham Foundation is gratefully acknowledged. It was a significant help in the planning stages of the project. Also acknowledged is the volunteer work of the many contributors to this Monograph. Their effort is what made this volume a reality.

Marcy Li Wang, Chairman
Isao Sakamoto, Vice Chairman
Bruce L. Bassler, Editor

Contents

Cladding

1

Cladding Systems and Materials

1.1 THE ADVENT AND PURPOSE OF CLADDING

Preindustrial-age buildings were commonly constructed with massive load bearing walls, which constituted both structure and thermal barrier. These buildings functioned environmentally well. In cold climates, masonry fireplaces generated and stored heat during the day and radiated their warmth through the building at night long after the fire had died. On hot days, buildings provided shade while the thermal lag of the massive walls tempered the interior temperature from the hot external climate.

The dominance of such buildings through much of history resulted not only from the limits of available materials but also from the state of pre-Industrial Revolution technology. The relatively few building types were constructed by craftspersons who knew and understood the characteristics of the locally available materials and the methods of installing them. What evolved were building techniques which were well adapted to the climatic conditions. A good knowledge of material properties enabled ordinary builders to design and construct buildings which satisfied esthetic, environmental, and physical concerns.

The development of cast-iron and steel-framed structures in the nineteenth century, followed by reinforced concrete–framed structures, signaled the end to the predominance of massive load-bearing systems. Architects and engineers found themselves liberated by new technologies of the structural frame, and they began to invent methods of enclosure, which were needed to complete the system. Steel and concrete frames could provide structure to deal with gravity and lateral loads of unprecedented heights. A building enclosure, extrinsic to the structural frame, would then provide the skin of the building—to protect the interior from the outside elements and to provide the most important visual component of the building exterior. These tall buildings, which took advantage of steel or concrete frames, provided building users with an abundance of light and panoramic views—amenities unavailable with the massive load bearing wall buildings. Facades with opportunities for expansive glazing came into being. *Cladding* was born.

In the twentieth century, building types, materials, and methods emerged at an accelerating rate. This development had a serious drawback: a less-than-comprehensive understanding of materials and methods along with the develop-

1

ment of codes, regulations, and standard tests replaced the empirical methods craftspersons had used in designing and constructing buildings. To satisfy the modern pace of innovation, a certain level of competence in design and construction was lost. The failure of many building envelopes can often be traced to the general lack of an emphasis toward the multitude of detailing decisions which affect the design. Inappropriate applications of technology did more to create problems with modern architecture than any other aspect of design. At worst, a designer's willingness to have the form of the building and its components dictated by manufacturing and production considerations often resulted in buildings that were esthetically successful when new but were later marred by leaks, progressive streaking, staining, and discoloration—the results of improper cladding details.

Some cladding materials used in current practices, such as the exterior insulation and finish system (EIFS) and large ceramic cladding panels [1600 by 1250 by 8 mm (63.0 by 49.3 by 0.3 in.) thick], were once unique to Europe, and Japanese engineers have recently introduced innovative ceramic and glass cladding materials, which are already having a global impact on the design of tall buildings. In addition, Japan has proven itself as a leader in the use of the open-joint (rain-screen) principle, which eliminates exterior primary seals. Examples of some of these innovations are described in Chapter 6.

The subsequent chapters of this volume build on topics covered in the *Monograph on Tall Building Systems and Concepts,* one of a series of monographs of the Council on Tall Buildings and Urban Habitat published by the American Society of Civil Engineers in 1980 (Council on Tall Buildings, Group SC, 1980).

1.2 MATERIALS AND FINISHES

The exterior material of the cladding system is the first, and sometimes only, defense against water penetration and other environmental conditions. It also significantly defines the esthetics of the building. We must carefully analyze the ability of the material and its attachment method to resist deterioration caused by severe weather, freeze/thaw cycling in colder climates, high temperature and humidity in warmer climates, and unique factors such as pollution in large cities or industrial areas.

Materials used for cladding tall buildings fall into six general categories. These are cementitious, masonry, stone, metal, glass, and plastic. Within each general category many subcategories exist. The following information attempts to identify these subcategories and provide design criteria for their selection and use.

1 Cementitious Materials

Materials which have cement as their primary binder are referred to as cementitious materials. They may be cast-in-place or precast concrete with a wide variety of admixtures, reinforcing, stucco, and plaster-type materials, or cementitious boards. Not included are concrete blocks, which fall into the masonry category, and synthetic plaster systems, which may contain cement but have as their primary binder a polymeric resin that falls into the plastic category.

Concrete is a mixture of cement, water, and an inert graded aggregate. When initially mixed, it is in a paste or fluidlike state, and after a short period of time hardens into a rigid mass. There are many admixtures which can alter or enhance the property of the concrete during placing or in its final form. These fall into four commonly used forms. Accelerators and reducers vary the time required for the concrete to cure; reducers also increase its workability without reducing its strength. Polymers and air entrainments enhance the strength and durability of the concrete. The selection of the aggregate affects strength and freeze/thaw resistance and is influenced by limitations of size due to placement dimensions of the member, reinforcement, and clearances around the reinforcement.

Reinforcement is added to concrete to enhance the ability of the material to resist tensile and shear stresses caused by loading and stresses induced by volumetric changes due to temperature and shrinkage. The reinforcement may be in the form of fibers, wire mesh, plain and deformed bars, or post- and pretensioned cables. Post- and pretensioned cables decrease the amount of concrete required, increase the load-carrying capacity, and reduce the possibility of load-induced cracking. Fiber reinforcing may be steel, glass, or plastic and is normally used as secondary reinforcement to control shrinkage and the associated cracking. Fiber reinforcing also increases flexure, tensile, and impact strengths, making it ideal for reinforcing thin facing panels. Mica flakes are used as a form of fiber reinforcing for boards, facing panels, and pipes to replace mineral fibers in products formerly known as cement asbestos.

Concrete is normally classified by the type of placement (cast-in-place or precast) and the type of reinforcement (conventional, prestressed, or fiber). Cast-in-place concrete can be used as exterior cladding, but the majority of cladding is architectural precast concrete. A wide range of esthetic expressions is available by varying the shape of the mold along with the color and texture of the exposed surface. The design of the precast wall panel involves more than just the selection of the exterior appearance. In-service, handling, and erection loads must be analyzed, properties of the concrete mixture and reinforcement must be determined, and connections to the building and means for handling and erecting the panel must be designed and detailed. The responsibility for these design aspects is usually divided among architect, structural engineer, and precaster. The architect and the engineer are normally responsible for the in-service loads, while the precaster is responsible for handling and erection. Cooperation in the design of connections and exterior appearance is imperative. The architect will usually specify the general exterior appearance, while the details for achieving that appearance are left to the precaster, who is experienced in working with additives for color or texture and in developing shapes, corners, and joints to avoid problems during casting or erection.

Guidelines for the design and erection of architectural precast concrete are discussed in *Structural Design in Architectural Precast Concrete,* published by the Prestressed Concrete Institute (PCI, 1977). Specifications, standards, and codes for precast concrete wall panels are found in publications of the American Concrete Institute (ACI 318, 1989; 533, 1965).

The tensile strength of concrete is low compared to its compressive strength; therefore design emphasis for concrete components is on minimizing tensile stresses. Such stresses, however, invariably do occur in flexure, diagonal tension, or due to differential strains. Where they occur, tensile stresses are expected to be carried entirely by steel reinforcing bars. Because one of the consequences for tensile stresses in concrete is cracking, which can lead to a decrease in durability, any technique that can provide concrete with greater tensile strength and "ductility" would be very valuable. One relatively new development is fiber-reinforced concrete (FRC).

FRC is a combination of portland cement (with or without aggregates of various sizes) and discrete fibers, including steel, glass, organic polymers, ceramics, and other organic materials. Steel fibers may be produced by either cutting wire, shearing sheets, or hot-melt extraction. They may be smooth or deformed to improve the bond. They can rust at the surface of the concrete, but appear to be very durable within the concrete mass. Glass fibers are generally available as "chopped strand," where each strand may consist of 100 to 400 separate filaments. A new fiber, Kevlar, which is an aromatic polyamide, has both a high tensile strength and a high modulus of elasticity. It shows considerable promise as reinforcement but is currently very expensive.

There are a number of ways of introducing fibers into a concrete mix. For short fibers (normally steel or glass), which are supposed to achieve a random orientation, standard concrete mixers may be used. With this method, only about 3% by volume of fibers can be added, and the problem to avoid is "balling up" of the fibers, particularly steel. This can be overcome most easily by mixing all the other ingredients and then adding the fibers gradually. Steel fibers may have to be vibrated through a coarse screen or otherwise separated.

For glass fibers, a "spray-up" method is often used to produce thin sheets. Using a special pump and spray gun, the fibers are chopped and combined with a cement slurry and then sprayed onto a mold. This method can also be used with carbon and other organic fibers, and can introduce about 10% by volume of fibers. For obtaining a more efficient fiber orientation, the winding process may be used with continuous fibers or filaments. The fibers are passed through a cement slurry, then wound on a frame. Additional slurry and chopped fiber may then be sprayed on to achieve the desired thickness. With this method, up to 15% by volume of fibers can be achieved.

It should be noted that the mix proportions for FRC are not the same as those for ordinary concrete. Higher cement contents are generally used for FRC to provide enough paste to coat the fibers, and pozzolans are a useful way of increasing the paste content without increasing the cement. Higher air content is needed because of the high paste content, but the percentage of air in the paste need not be higher. The maximum aggregate size is generally 10 mm (0.4 in.), and a fairly high ratio of fine to coarse aggregate is used.

Durability is as important as strength in determining the suitability of concrete for any specific application. Durable concrete should generally be dense and impermeable. The porosity of FRC, however, appears to be higher than that of plain concrete because of difficulties in fully compacting the mix. Because FRC is a fairly recent development, few long-term durability data are available.

If steel FRC is made with an appropriate paste content and water-cement ratio for the exposure condition in question, the alkaline environment in an uncracked state provides adequate protection for the fibers. Once the concrete cracks, however, particularly in a marine or acid environment, the rate of corrosion and carbonation will increase considerably and surface rusting will occur. While this is only a cosmetic effect, the magnitude of the corrosion is contingent on the quantity of available moisture.

Glass-fiber-reinforced concrete (GFRC) may indeed be the material of the future for building cladding when the design concept calls for the appearance of mass and durability not found in metal or glass cladding systems. The advantages of GFRC are reduced weight, added flexure, tensile, and impact strengths, and possible cost savings due to reduced weight and construction time. The reduced-weight cost savings are expected to be realized in the cost of foundations, exterior framing, erection equipment, and fastening systems. GFRC also allows the designer great flexibility in shapes and finishes.

As with many new cladding systems, GFRC was not without problems when it was introduced. One of these problems was the durability of the glass fiber when exposed to the alkaline portland cement. Alkali-resistant glass fibers were first developed in 1969 and seem to be performing well. However, with time, even alkali-resistant glass fibers are attacked by the alkaline cement; thus, the designer must take into account a loss of strength as the material ages.

Standards for the design and use of *fiber-reinforced concrete* can be found in Subsection 2 of Section 1.6.

Stucco and exterior plastic are field-mixed and -applied materials composed of cement, aggregate, and water. The cement may be portland, masonry, or gypsum, and the aggregate is usually sand. Several types of admixtures are available for use with stucco and plaster materials. These include plasticizers, air entrainments, accelerators, water repellents, bonding agents, and coloring pigments. The use of admixtures should always be checked through laboratory analysis or past performance to ensure that adverse effects will not occur. These materials can be applied with hand trowels or spray equipment directly to cementitious and masonry substrates or over stud walls with metal lath and wire reinforcement. Wide variations in both color and texture can be achieved with the placement of the finish coat.

Careful attention in both the design and the installation of joint locations, placement, and reinforcing will prevent cracking. In general, control joints should be placed at all changes in the material to which stucco is applied, and large areas should be divided into relatively square panels having a maximum area of 14 m^2 (150 ft^2) and a maximum dimension of 3 m (10 ft).

Standards for the design and use of *stucco* can be found in Subsection 3 of Section 1.6.

2   Masonry Materials

The design of masonry cladding for tall modern buildings requires careful and special consideration. As discussed, early buildings were built with massive load-bearing walls. These walls were usually constructed of masonry or stone and reacted very differently than the thin veneer walls typically used for cladding buildings today. Unfortunately, some designers' knowledge of masonry properties is based on the use of masonry as a thick solid wall, not a thin veneer. Compressive strength is no longer the most important property of the conventional masonry wall, which is capable of supporting its own weight for heights of 30 m (100 ft) of more. The weatherability of the masonry units, the tensile strength of the bond with the mortar, the stiffness of the support wall, and the means of tying the units together takes on much more importance as the designer tries to avoid problems.

Some of the most prevalent problems with the masonry veneers used for cladding on tall buildings are:

1. Lack of provision for the volumetric changes which will occur in the masonry unit, back-up support system, and primary structural system

2. Lack of proper detailing of the means to prevent water from infiltrating into the building through the cladding
3. Lack of proper understanding and failure to analyze the relative stiffness of the exterior masonry and the back-up support system

Design information covering the first two of these problems is presented in Chapter 2. Information on the design of the entire wall assembly is more complex than can be presented here. The use of steel studs as the support framing for masonry veneers is the subject of controversy in the design and construction industry. The Brick Institute of America's Technical Note 28B discusses this system at length (BIA, 1987). The system was tested and reported on by Clemson University in 1982, and the Masonry Advisory Council in Park Ridge, Illinois, has published at least 12 *Design Alerts* (1987) regarding the system. The best advice that can be given a designer is to study the information contained in these documents, stay current with all new information, and make decisions accordingly.

Other suggested references for *brick construction* are given in Subsection 4 of Section 1.6.

Similar to brick, concrete block is manufactured in a wide variety of textures, shapes, and finishes. Technical information is available through the National Concrete Masonry Association (NCMA), which publishes a series of technical notes entitled NCMA-TEK. Because concrete block is manufactured by pouring a cementitious mixture into molds and curing by air drying or steam and pressure curing, it is not as impervious to moisture penetration as fired clay brick. The NCMA recommends that a waterproof coating be applied to concrete unit masonry walls in most geographic locations.

Other suggested references for *concrete unit masonry construction* are given in Subsection 5 of Section 1.6.

Cavity walls are the most effective system for resisting the penetration of rain. Single-withe and double-withe concrete unit facade walls without cavities for drainage are used widely in all parts of the country. Flexure, tensile, and shear strength of mortar joints containing flashing cannot be utilized according to ACI 530.1 Limitations are also suggested on mortar joint tooling. Concave and V-shaped mortar joints are considered to be best. Beaded, weathered, flush, raked, extruded, and struck joints are less desirable. Masonry facade walls, whether or not they contain a cavity, should be constructed with weep holes and flashings. Careful detailing of flashings is essential so as not to compromise wall strength (Fig. 1.1).

One of the significant differences between the recommendations of the American Society for Testing and Materials, ASTM C270 (1989) and ASTM C476 (1983), for concrete unit masonry and the recommendations of the Brick Institute of America for clay unit masonry is that ASTM C270 and C476 allow the use of masonry cement. Before using masonry cement, however, all applicable codes should also be checked. Some building codes require that the air content of all mortars not exceed 12%, and mortars made with masonry cement often will not satisfy this requirement. Another significant difference between brick and block is the manner in which they respond to moisture. Brick expands when its moisture content increases, and this is not reversible during drying, whereas initial drying shrinkage occurs with concrete unit masonry. This initial drying shrinkage is greater than the normal expansion and contraction due to fluctuations in moisture content from atmospheric conditions.

Glass block was developed in 1929 and first manufactured in 1933. Having been very popular in the Art Deco period of the 1930s, it has reappeared in recent years as an exterior wall finish. It can be manufactured in a wide variety of styles: hollow or solid, clear or opaque, and geometric or free-form patterns. Hollow blocks are manufactured of two pressed-glass shapes fused together into a single unit at elevated temperatures, after which the air in the hollow space is dehydrated and partially evacuated. Both hollow and solid blocks are made of glass with a general chemical composition similar to that of sheet glass materials.

The use of glass block as an exterior wall material is limited in length, height, and square foot area, depending on the edge restraint of the panel. The *Basic Building Code* of Building Officials and Code Administrators International (BOCA, 1990) gives the following limitations for structural glass block walls:

> **1408.1 Exterior wall panels:** The maximum dimensions of glass block wall panels in exterior walls, when used singly or in multiples forming continuous bands of structural glass block between structural supports, shall be 25 feet in length and 20 feet in height between structural supports and expansion joints; and the area of each individual panel shall be not more than 250 square feet. Intermediate structural support shall be provided to support the dead load of the wall and all other superimposed loads. Where individual panels are more than 144 square feet in area, a supplementary stiffener shall be provided to anchor the panels to the structural support.

The same code gives the following requirements for mortar, reinforcements, and sealants:

> **1408.2 Joint materials:** Glass blocks shall be laid up in Type S or N mortar with approved galvanized or other noncorrosive metal wall ties in the horizontal mortar joints of exterior panels. The sills of glass block panels shall be coated with approved asphaltic emulsion, or other elastic waterproofing material, previous to laying the first mortar course, and the perimeter of the panels shall be caulked to a depth of not less than ½ inch with nonhardening caulking compound on both faces; or other approved expansion joints shall be provided. When laid up in joint materials other than mortars herein defined, a single panel shall not be more than 100 square feet in area, nor more than 10 feet in either length or height.

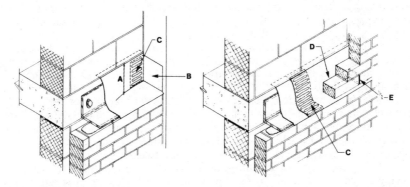

Fig. 1.1 Flashing a masonry cavity: A = adequate height [usually 203 mm (8 in.)]; B = end dams to contain water; C = sealed seams with mastic of sealant; D = clean cavity (debris blocks weep hole); E = weep holes to drain water at proper spacing.

Suggested references and standards for *glass block* are given in Subsection 6 of Section 1.6.

3 Stone Materials

Similar to masonry, natural stone exterior finishes are used on today's modern buildings, particularly when a monumental design expression is desired. With rising construction costs, stone veneers have tended to decrease gradually in thickness to reduce the dead load imposed on the skeleton frame and the cost of construction. The use of thin stone veneers, less than 50 mm (2 in.) thick, is relatively new. Therefore, the behavior of many ultrathin stone veneers over a prolonged period of time has not been determined by actual use; but already, dramatic problems of stone failures as a result of thin veneer have occurred. Recent investigations of problems with thin stone veneer cladding indicate that improper and incomplete analyses of stress concentrations, connections, and joints as they relate to the physical properties of the stone have been responsible for distress and failures.

Stone varieties most commonly used for cladding buildings are granite, limestone, marble, sandstone, slate, and travertine. Because these materials are natural and not manufactured under rigid quality control standards, the physical property of any one variety will vary not only from quarry to quarry, but from different areas or levels in the same quarry. The finish of the stone can also influence the physical properties of the stone. A polished or honed finish maintains the strength of the stone, while thermal finishing or bush hammering produces microcracks in its surface, thus reducing the effective thickness. For these reasons, even the best analyzed designs must be reanalyzed after the actual stone with the specified finish has been tested to determine its physical properties. The most important physical property is the ability of the stone to withstand the stresses induced by the transmission of the dead, wind, and seismic loads to the anchors or connectors. Another property which must be considered is permeability and the ability of the stones to withstand chemical attack from acid rain, pollution, and the like.

Chemical attack on the stone cladding of many older monumental buildings is an area of widespread concern and study. The amount of moisture which can penetrate thin veneers is greater than with the thicker materials used in the past. This increased penetration affects freeze/thaw cycling as well as the effects of weathering on the strength of the stone unit.

Although empirical design procedures are published in standards such as ANSI A41.1 (1953), most cladding design is based on a rational analysis of the flexure strength of the stone. Laboratory testing of various stone materials indicates that the flexure strengths can vary with age and exposure to normal heat/cool or freeze/thaw cycles. Because of this, the safety factors for the design of stone cladding must be higher than for other common building materials. These safety factors, recommended by trade associations and suppliers, can range from 3 for granite to 5 for marble subjected to concentrated loads.

Attachment systems for stone vary with the thickness of the stone and the type of support system used. Stones of 75- to 100-mm (3- to 4-in.) thickness are usually supported by shelf angles, whereas thinner stones are attached by continuous or individual clips set into kerfs in the ends of the stone. While many codes and specifications now require positive mechanical anchorage, some attachment systems rely on the adhesive bonding of a piece of stone to the substrate or subsystem. This procedure is receiving considerable criticism because of the risk of bond failure in blind anchorages. The calculation of the bending stress induced in the stone by the service loads is fairly simple for continuous clip angles completely around the stone and complex for individual clips not located at the corners. This latter calculations must take into account the physical dimensions and shapes of the kerf.

Stone cladding is no different than other cladding materials in terms of control of water, design of joints, and provision for not overstressing the material when it is handled prior to installation. The designer must recognize that a certain amount of water will penetrate through the veneer under wind-driven rain conditions, that condensation could develop on the back side of the veneer, and that consequently a second line of defense in the form of flashings and weep holes should be provided in thin stone veneers to collect the water and divert it to the exterior of the building. To prevent unanticipated stresses and associated distress from developing in stone veneers attached to the structural frames, it is essential that properly sized horizontal expansion joints be located between stone panels and below supporting steel clip angles to allow the structure to shorten and deflect and the stone veneer to expand and contract. Like precast concrete, large handling stresses can occur when stone is transported lying flat and when it is lifted from a horizontal position. Other handling loads can occur from accidental impact and from the stone being forced into tight locations. Although handling loads are sometimes difficult to define, their effects must be considered and addressed in design. Previous industry standards established minimum thickness requirements for stone veneers, based on past practice. These requirements helped to prevent damage from some handling load conditions, particularly jarring and vibration from vehicular transport. Contemporary practice, however, is to minimize the thickness. Kerf loading and anchor stresses exerted on the stone become the critical criteria for thickness selection, even with adequate thickness for wind loading. Experience indicates that 10 mm (0.4 in.) is the realistic minimum thickness for unbonded stone veneer.

Some of the references and standards available for *stone materials* are given in Subsection 7 of Section 1.6.

4 Metal Materials

One of the earliest recorded uses of metal cladding was in the 1860s in New York City, when James Bogardus bolted cast-iron panels to cast-iron structures on five- or six-story buildings. Metal cladding used today falls into three basic categories: plate, laminated sheet, and sandwich panels, and utilizes either steel or aluminum as the exterior material.

Plate types can be as thin as 26-gauge steel or 0.813-mm (1/31-in.) aluminum, which are used in combination with different types and styles of backer framing and girts to create a built-up panel in the field, or as thick as 6.4 mm (1/4 in.) to be used as independently attached panels. Laminated sheet panels are manufactured by laminating metal sheets to a thin solid noninsulating core with or without a metal interior liner. Typical materials used for the core in laminated sheet panels are plywood, hardboard, particle board, gypsum board, cement board, and thermoplastic. Sandwich panels are manufactured by facing both sides of a rigid insulation or nonsolid core, such a paper or metal honeycomb, with metal sheets.

Sandwich panels are manufactured with foamed-in-place insulation and by hot-pressure laminating. The *R* values of insulated sandwich panels vary with the type and thickness of the insulation and can be as high as 28.5.

Most metal cladding is installed as a curtain wall, either in an exposed grid frame or back-fastened to an interior girt frame system. Some manufacturers design, supply, and erect the grid and girt frame system, while others only manufacture the metal cladding in sheet or panel form to be installed on frames designed, supplied, and installed by others.

When the panels are set in an exposed grid, the edges set in the frame are sealed to the frame and the frame is finished in a similar way as the panel. When the panels are installed on interior girt framing, the joints between the panels may be butted, lapped, interlocked, splined, or covered with a batten. Each one of these types of joints has an individual configuration and requires a different sealant or gasket design to perform properly as a watertight exterior cladding. With the exception of stainless steels and weathering steels, such as Cor-ten from U.S. Steel, which need no exterior finish for areas exposed to view, metal claddings are painted or anodized. Coatings are recommended for concealed areas when weathering steels are used.

Suggested references and standards for *metal cladding materials* are given in Subsection 8 of Section 1.6, as well as in publications by the American Society for Testing and Materials and Underwriters Laboratories.

5 Glass Materials

With the advent of the structural frame came the desire for buildings that were light and airy in appearance through the use of transparent glass walls. An early dramatic illustration of this type of design was John Paxton's Crystal Palace, built in 1851 for London's Exposition. Willis Polk's Hallidie Building, built in San Francisco in 1917, is considered by many to be the first glass curtain-wall facade.

As used today for the exterior cladding on tall buildings, glass is usually installed in a curtain-wall-type frame, or in window frames in other types of exterior cladding systems and materials. The designer must not only determine the type of glass, but also the framing, seals, and gaskets, which must be properly selected and specified. Because windows and most glass curtain-wall systems are manufactured items, the manufacturer's engineers and designers will take the responsibility for these items when the building designer specifies the criteria for structural, water penetration, air leakage, thermal, light, and sound-transmission performance, fire resistance, and provision for thermal movements. The Architectural Aluminum Manufacturers' Association (AAMA) publishes the *Guide Specifications Manual* (AAMA 1987), which can be used by the building designer to develop the curtain-wall specification. It also sponsors the "Voluntary Specifications for Aluminum Prime Windows" (AAMA, 1987), which can be used as a guide for preparing specifications for aluminum frame windows.

The designer has many options in glass selection and glazing design to meet functional, safety, and esthetic requirements for a particular building. The choice for a particular facade design should be based on several considerations, including type and thickness of the glass to meet wind-load requirements, hazard potential from glass breakage, breakage potential resulting from differential heat gain or loss, thermal insulation requirements, solar gain (greenhouse effect), fire safety, appearance, and cost.

Glass used for exterior cladding is manufactured with a variety of additives and combinations of layers, which develop different characteristics of strength, appearance, and thermal and visual performance. All glass is a product of fusing inorganic materials, such as silicon, sodium, and calcium, into a liquid ceramic material which, when cooled without crystallization, is transparent, hard, brittle, and chemically inert. Glass can be colored by adding other materials, which are primarily metal oxides polarized with an organic crystalline chemical, tempered by heat to increase strength, and patterned by etching, sandblasting, or passing it through a pair of rolls with designs on them. Strength, insulating, heat-absorbing, and glare-reducing properties can also be changed by varying the chemical makeup or by combining sheets of glass and adding different films or coatings. The designer must specify the performance characteristics of the glass carefully.

Most buildings being constructed today utilize multiple-pane insulating glass. This type of glazing is manufactured by combining two or three sheets of glass with an air space between them. The edges of the air space are sealed with a primary and a secondary seal to prevent moisture accumulation between the sheets. Most manufacturers will warrant these seals for a period of 10 years.

Suggested references and standards for *glass* are provided in Subsection 9 of Section 1.6.

Crystallized glass panels were developed in Japan in the early 1970s and are manufactured by combining a special formulation of the raw materials used to make glass. The combination is melted, crushed, granulated in water, and dried prior to being heated to fuse the granules together in the form of needle-shaped crystals. The panels are then ground smooth, producing a fine gloss and pattern surface. The resulting material resembles marble in appearance and has greater strength and weather resistance than granite. The maximum panel size currently available is approximately 900 by 1200 mm (3 by 4 ft). The material is professed to be 30% lighter than stone and to have an absorption rate of 0.00%. Panels can be reheated and formed into curved surfaces with a gentle and soft texture.

6 Plastic Materials

Plastic is a classification to which no strictly scientific definition can be applied. It is a product of synthetic origin, which is capable of being shaped by flow in some stage of manufacture, and which is not rubber, wood, leather, or metal. Plastics were first thought to be a synthetic building material that would answer all the difficulties encountered in existing materials. This belief resulted in great disillusionment as the early plastics had not been tested adequately.

Plastics used for exterior cladding today fall into the general categories of sheet plastics and polymer modifiers. Sheet plastics are used as alternate materials for glass and metal siding. As a replacement for glass, plastic can be clear polycarbonate or patterned and textured to create dramatic esthetic expressions. Each manufacturer can provide the designer with test data on strength, impact resistance, weatherability, fire, and other properties, which must be considered when selecting a material for a specific use. As a replacement for metal siding, plastic sheets can be manufactured in flat or corrugated shapes and in a wide variety of colors. Because of its ability to reproduce ornate designs for columns, relief panels, and ornamentation at a lower cost than the carved stone which was used in the past, plastic will continue to show potential for the future.

The largest use of polymer modifiers in exterior cladding today is in the production of exterior insulation finish systems (EIFS). Most EIFS systems consist of a polymer or polymer-modified cement applied over rigid foam-board insulation which is attached to the building. Most of the early systems used in the United States in the 1970s were of European origin. The best known one is from Dryvit System, Inc. It was developed in Germany in 1947 and introduced in the United States in 1969. EIFS systems are receiving wide acceptance for new buildings and retrofitting because of relatively low cost, attractive appearance, and thermal insulation on the outside of the building, eliminating a thermal impact to the structural system. Most manufacturers have developed reinforcing meshes and hard-coat systems which help in hardening the exterior surface and increase the impact resistance.

1.3　COMPONENTS

All cladding systems consist of six basic components. First there is the exterior material, which has already been discussed. The other five components include support framing, interior finish, insulation, joint treatment, and internal drainage. Some types of cladding systems contain all of these components as a package, such as metal and glass curtain walls, where the manufacturer, supplier, and erector take the responsibility for these components under a single performance specification. Other cladding systems may contain some of these components as a package, while still others require the designer to select and specify each component separately (Fig. 1.2).

1　Support Framing

Regardless of the type of exterior material selected for the cladding, it must have some form of framing. This support framing holds the exterior material to the building and transfers the loads imposed on the exterior material by wind, dead weight, and seismic forces to the structural frame. The support frame must also

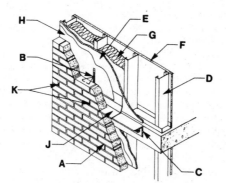

Fig. 1.2　Components, brick veneer over steel stud wall. *Exterior material*: A = brick; B = tie to support frame. *Support framing*: C = shelf angle; D = steel stud; E = sheathing; F = interior drywall. *Insulation*: G = batt insulation. *Interior finish*: F = interior drywall. *Joints*: K = sealant between weep holes. *Internal drainage*: H = building paper; J = flashing; K = weep holes.

be able to accommodate the differences in movement of the exterior material, the support framing, and the structural frame caused by moisture and temperature expansion and contraction, the structural frame creep and shrinkage, and the drift or movement of the structural frame caused by wind or earthquakes.

The support framing for precast concrete panels is integral to the exterior material in the form of reinforcements and built-in attachments. The support frame for manufacturer-designed glass and metal panel curtain walls is integral to the design in the form of mullions and girts which frame the panels. When glass and metal panel curtain walls are specified to be designed by a manufacturer using a performance specification, the building designer usually needs to design only the attachment of the mullion and girt frame system to the structural frame. Manufacturers and suppliers of other exterior materials, such as GFRC, synthetic plaster systems, plate and laminated metal panels, or reinforced brick panel systems, also include the design of the support framing.

When using laid-in-place masonry and stone materials, or when the building designer actually designs the wall system utilizing any of the other exterior materials, the designer must select and design the support framing. There are two basic types of support framing: the grid-type frame and the back-up wall. The grid-type frame is more commonly used for glass and metal panel exterior materials. However, it is possible to attach other exterior materials, such as stone and prefabricated panels of masonry, metal plate, synthetic plaster, and GFRC, to grid-type frames. The grid frame is normally aluminum extrusion or structural steel shapes attached to the structural frame of the building with provisions for attachment of the exterior material. The back-up wall is itself an enclosure wall onto which the exterior material is attached. The two most common types of back-up walls are masonry and sheathed stud walls. Precast concrete has been used in some cases as a back-up wall; however, due to its weight and ability to also be the exterior material, it is rarely used unless the back-up wall is used as a portion of the structural frame.

The masonry back-up wall is normally laid-in-place concrete block with the exterior material attachments built into the wall as the wall is constructed. Usually these walls are of the infill type, built between the floors and exterior columns of the building. In addition to the built-in attachments, many times a shelf angle is attached to the structural slab to carry the weight of the exterior material, allowing the attachment system to be designed to resist only the horizontal loads imposed by wind or earthquake forces.

The steel-stud back-up wall is a framing system which came into use in the 1960s and 1970s. It is basically an adaptation of the brick over wood-stud construction used successfully on residential construction for decades. The advantages of this type of framing are that it is lightweight, easy to install, and capable of being prefabricated and panelized. This framing system has been severely criticized, particularly when used as backup for brick masonry. Often these criticisms are based on actual problems or failures which have occurred; however, it is the authors' opinion that when properly designed, detailed, and constructed, the steel-stud back-up framing system will perform satisfactorily.

The designer must consider the deflection of the stud or composite stud wall when selecting studs for a given project. This deflection must be compared to the allowable deflection of the exterior material being used. Stucco and cement plaster materials can usually withstand deflections up to L 360, where L is the distance between joints or points of zero deflection. In other words, a 3.6-m (12-ft) panel can be allowed to deflect 10 mm (0.4 in.) without causing cracking in the stucco or cement plaster. Calculations of structural properties of light-gauge steel members are normally based on the American Iron and Steel Institute "Specification for the Design of Cold-Rolled Formed Structural Members" (AISI, 1980). However, most manufacturers publish complete load tables which are convenient to use. Deflection limits based on composite action with facing materials are sometimes used by the manufacturer. These published limits, based on tests, will sometimes permit a reduction in the steel member size or gauge as opposed to determination solely by calculation.

The steel stud has received its most severe criticism when used as a back-up frame for brick masonry. Some metal-stud design tables are based on deflections of L 240 or L 360, which may permit more deflection than the brick wall can tolerate without breaking the bond between brick and mortar. The Brick Institute of America suggests a maximum deflection of L 600 to L 720 for steel-stud framing used to support a brick masonry wall. Even these higher limits have been questioned by some engineers. A designer who intends to use this type of framing should obtain the latest information on its use and design accordingly.

Suggested references for the design of *steel-stud support framing* are given in Subsection 10 of Section 1.6. Suggested references for the design of curtain-wall framing are the same as those listed in Subsection 8 of Section 1.6.

2 Interior Finishes

The interior finish on the cladding is normally an architectural treatment applied to the interior face of the support framing or a separate wall to achieve the degree of finishing desired for the space and is not related to the performance of the cladding. Exceptions to this are drywall used as lateral support for the interior face of steel-stud back-up framing and drywall or other finish material integral to the insulation and vapor barrier system.

3 Insulation

Current trends in energy conservation, mandated by codes and the energy-conscious society, have led to an increased use of better insulations in building cladding systems. Some of the cladding materials, such as insulated metal sandwich panels and the synthetic plasters over rigid insulation, contain the insulation inherently. Other materials, such as precast concrete and GFRC, can be manufactured with insulation sandwiched into the panel. Other types of cladding systems need to have the insulation added in the form of batts, blankets, rigid board, or fill. In addition to the standard construction types of insulation listed here, designers should begin to investigate the use of hybrid insulation blankets as used in other industries. For instance, the National Aeronautics and Space Administration uses blanket insulation with an R value of approximately 24 per 25-mm (1.0-in.) thickness and fire resistance up to 980°C (1800°F).

Blankets and batts can be inserted into framing systems like steel studs or surface-applied to solid walls such as precast concrete. The most common type of material used for this kind of insulation is fiberglass. Manufactured in varying widths, with or without a kraft-paper or foil vapor barrier, it can be either friction-fitted into the stud spaces or attached with tape or pins. The insulation value of fiberglass insulation is approximately $R = 3.1$ per 25 mm (1 in.).

Rigid board insulation used in modern construction is usually extruded or expanded foam insulation available in a wide variety of sizes and thicknesses. It can be placed in cavity spaces or adhered to the inside of solid back-up framing. In the latter case, some form of metal or wood furring is also installed to facilitate the installation of the interior wall finish. Extruded-foam insulation boards are more dense than expanded-foam boards and can better resist impact. Their insulation value is approximately $R = 5.4$ per 25 mm (1 in.), whereas the insulation value of expanded foam is approximately $R = 4.2$ per 25 mm (1 in.). Other types of board utilizing polyisocyanurate foam can achieve insulation values ranging to $R = 8.0$ per 25 mm (1 in.) of thickness.

Along with increased amounts of insulation, modern designs have included provisions to reduce the infiltration of unconditioned air into the building. This has created buildings with interior temperature, humidity, and pressure conditions considerably different from the exterior environment. The result of these greater differences is condensation on interior finishes and concealed spaces within the wall systems. In order to avoid these condensation problems, the dew-point locations must be analyzed using the interior and exterior extremes of temperature and humidity.

Single-material claddings, such as aluminum and glass curtain walls and windows, need to be broken thermally to prevent transfer of cold through the members. Cold interior surface temperatures in the window are the normal cause of condensation on these assemblies. The use of insulation usually requires the use of an air and vapor barrier to prevent the passage of moisture vapor to the location of the dew-point temperature, where it will condense and damage the materials. Vapor barriers are films of materials which have a vapor permeance ratio of 1 perm or less. Some examples are polyethylene films, foil backing on gypsum board, and specially formulated paints. The vapor barrier must be continuous with no open seams, gaps, or tears which would allow the passage of air. The most common locations for these voids in the vapor barrier are outlet boxes or other penetrations of the interior wall and unsealed voids at the tops and bottoms of walls or where framing members penetrate the vapor barrier. A well-designed vapor barrier of the highest-quality material can be rendered totally ineffective by the presence of only a few of these openings. The use of double vapor barriers on each side of the insulation can also be the cause of serious condensation within the wall.

4 Joints

Joints are used in cladding for two primary purposes. There are joints for ease of construction, such as between pieces of panelized systems, and joints provided to compensate for movement. A complete discussion on joints and sealants can be found in Chapter 2.

5 Internal Drainage

An owner expects the wall to permit no water to penetrate its exterior surface and damage the interior. The wall must permit any moisture within it to escape through the outer surface to the atmosphere. This cannot be achieved by the cladding material alone because there is no surfacing material with the unique characteristic of one-way permeability. Perhaps it is time for designers to examine the potential for using materials such as Gore-Tex® in conjunction with other surfacing materials to produce a breathable cladding system. Rain in combination with high winds can cause water to move over a wall surface in unpredictable directions. This water tends to find its way to and collect at the joints. Experience has shown that to provide a permanently waterproof seal only at the wall joints' outer surface is often not sufficient because of failures in workmanship or continual skin movement. A second line of defense is required. One method which has been used to prevent leakage in metal curtain walls is referred to as the *internal drainage system,* a method used for many years in the design of windows.

The internal drainage system is designed on the premise that the wall *will leak,* but when it occurs, the water can be collected, prevented from reaching the interior finishes, and channeled to the exterior of the wall. This is accomplished by designing the wall with a system of flashing and collection devices which channel water to drainage outlets in the exterior face of the wall.

One method for collecting water that is penetrating the exterior joints or seals in cladding is to install a combination of gutters and drains behind the joints. On high-rise buildings, this type of drainage system can fail because the quantity of water accumulated in long drainage runs can be excessive. Good designs for tall buildings drain the gutters directly to the outdoors at regular intervals by means of weep holes.

Weep holes for internal drainage systems serve as drains for condensate, which may occur on cold surfaces within the wall as well as leakage. If not designed and constructed carefully, they can be points of entry for water penetration. Heavy storms can create pressure from high winds on a wall, which can force rainwater into the openings. This would not generally occur under normal rainfall conditions. Therefore they must be located such that penetration of wind-driven rain is prevented or backed up by baffles so that penetration will be substantially reduced and no damage will result.

The interior drainage system within the wall is intended to function only as a back-up system and should not be used as the primary method to control leakage. The proper detailing of joints and selection of sealants must always be the main protection against water penetration under normal conditions.

1.4 SYSTEMS

The cladding systems for tall buildings can be classified into three basic types, depending on how they are attached to the structural frame. The types are attached, curtain wall, and infill. The latter two have the potential of contributing to the structural integrity of the frame and should possibly be considered as a hybrid fourth type.

1 Attached System

This type of system has the exterior cladding attached directly to the structural frame in large panels which span one or more stories and one or more bays; or it is constructed on the frame with the back-up material usually resting on the slab and the exterior finish covering the structural frame. Examples of the attached panel system are precast concrete or steel-stud frames with an exterior finish which is lifted into place by cranes and then welded or bolted to attachments built into the structural frame. An example of the second type of attached cladding system would be a brick veneer wall in which the masonry or steel-stud back-up system is constructed on the slabs with the exterior brick veneer supported by shelf angles attached to the slab edges (Fig. 1.3).

The primary advantages of this type of system are the ability to fully insulate the exterior walls and protect the structural frame from the deteriorating effects of weather. The attached panel system has the added advantage of ease of erection and reduced construction time at the job site. This reduced construction time at the job site is sometimes offset by design, shop drawing approval, and manufacturing time on competitively bid projects, resulting in a total construction time from contract to occupancy roughly equal to or sometimes longer than that of

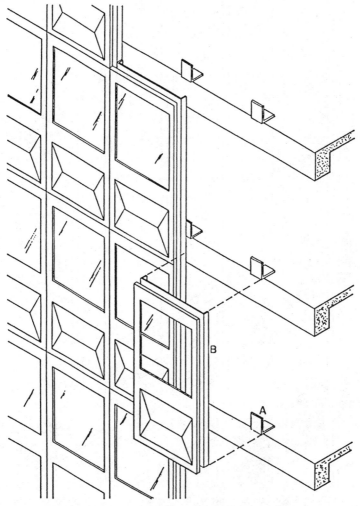

Fig. 1.3   Attached systems: A = anchor; B = attached panel.

nonpanelized construction. Differential movement must also be analyzed with this system in the design of joints and attachments to prevent future problems with leaks or deterioration of the cladding material.

2 Curtain-Wall System

This system is similar to the attached system except that it is attached to the structural frame with clip angles or subframing (Fig. 1.4). The most prevalent types of curtain-wall systems are the metal or metal and glass walls which en-

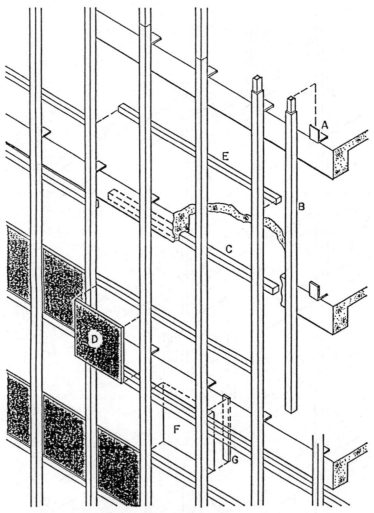

Fig. 1.4 Curtain-wall systems: A = anchor; B = mullion; C = cast-in-place rail; D = spandrel panel; E = horizontal rail; F = vision glass; G = interior trim.

close many of today's modern skyscrapers. Other materials, such as natural stones and lightweight precast panels, are also commonly used as cladding material for curtain-wall systems.

The advantages of this system are similar to those of the attached system, while affording the contractor or erector the ability to handle and erect smaller, lightweight pieces. These often are of standard design and manufacture, requiring less time in the preconstruction shop drawing and manufacturing phases of the project. When manufactured glass or metal curtain walls are used, the manufacturers normally design the joints and connections based on their intimate knowledge of the behavior of the system and materials and the structural frame characteristics supplied by the architect or structural engineer. Curtain-wall systems utilizing natural stone, precast concrete, or combinations of materials must be designed and detailed with joints and attachments by the architect to prevent problems caused by differential movement.

3 Infill System

This system is most representative of cast-in-place concrete structural frames. The cladding material is installed between the exterior floor slab edges, and sometimes the exterior columns of the structural frame are also exposed. The cladding material may be precast concrete, masonry, glass, or a combination of glass and another material at the windowsill or jambs. The identifying feature of this system is that the structural frame is exposed (Fig 1.5).

The primary advantage of this system is that it can be installed from the interior without relying on exterior scaffolding. Three disadvantages of this system are that the structural frame is difficult or impossible to insulate, the structural frame is exposed to the elements, and differential movement will occur between the exposed structural frame and the cladding. The lack of insulation on or in the structural floor slabs results in additional heat loss and heat gain to the interior environment. The exterior columns when exposed can usually be insulated on the interior. The exposure of the structural frame to the exterior with drastic changes in annual temperature and precipitation can cause problems, such as spalling concrete. Care must be taken in the selection, design, and construction of the exposed structural elements to avoid this problem. The third disadvantage of this system is related to the second, in that problems are caused by the different manners in which structure and cladding material react to the climate and change volume as they age.

4 Systems Which Contribute to the Structural Frame

Precast concrete panels, masonry walls, or even exposed cast-in-place exterior walls can be used to assist the structural system in resisting the effects of wind and seismic loads, and in some cases carry the live and dead loads of the building. When the cladding contributes to the structure, its joints and attachments must be designed to perform their structural function as well as accommodate the effects of differential movement.

1.5 SELECTION OF SYSTEM AND MATERIAL

The basic design criteria are environment, structural, cost, codes, esthetics, erection, and maintenance. Any single criterion or combinations of criteria may be used in the initial selection process. There is no single most important criterion which should influence this decision on every building because each building is designed for its own use on its own site.

1 Environmental Criteria

Environmental criteria are rarely considered by the designer to be primary and initial criteria. Since the energy crisis in the early 1970s, environmental perfor-

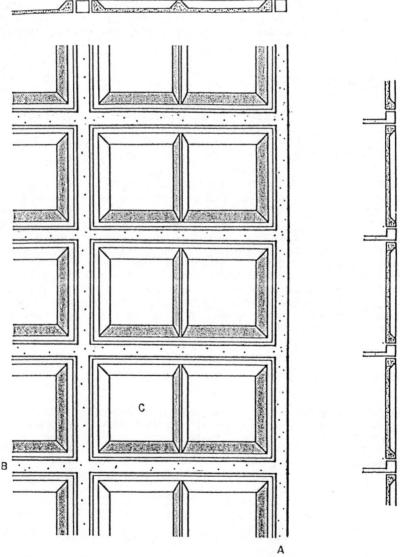

Fig. 1.5　Infill systems: A = exposed column; B = exposed slab; C = infill panel.

mance has become code mandated for energy conservation. These code requirements normally deal with performance of the insulation value and do not address
the other ways in which the environment affects the building and its users. The
cladding must act to filter or control the effects of rain, snow, sound, and pollution, as well as temperature fluctuations and extremes.

The most prevalent problem associated with the cladding of tall buildings is
moisture. A moisture problem can be caused by water penetration or condensation. Both sources of moisture can cause very serious problems, such as damage
to interior and exterior finish materials, failure of connections due to corrosion or
freeze/thaw forces, and loss of insulation performance. Water can penetrate the
cladding material on the building through joints which were improperly sealed,
sealant failures, or cracks in the exterior skin. Condensation, on the other hand,
is a result of the lack of a vapor barrier, faulty insulation, or a thermal break.
Surveys of residents in buildings experiencing extensive moisture problems often
reveal that the majority of the complaints result from condensation and icing on
single-glazing and metal windows without thermal breaks. With today's materials, technology, and design data, appropriate consideration of the exterior environment, the proposed interior environmental controls, and design of the cladding will avoid these problems.

Air infiltration through the exterior cladding is a result of the same failures
in the exterior skin; however, the problems caused are different. Air infiltration can be the cause of condensation and icing or it can cause inefficiencies in
the heating, ventilating, and air-conditioning (HVAC) system, resulting in
drafts, higher operating costs, and system balancing problems. Certain
amounts of air infiltration are considered acceptable, but these values must be
controlled and considered by the mechanical engineer when designing the
HVAC system and working with the other designers to select and locate the
insulation and vapor barriers.

Pollution may be in the form of dirt, which causes staining and disturbs the
esthetic appearance of the building, or it may be in the form of airborne contam-
inants, such as acid rain or chemical discharge from industry or transportation,
which may damage the finish material. If there is reason to believe that these conditions exist, it would be advisable to have a contamination survey made of the
site and consult a chemist or coatings expert before selecting a material to ensure
that it can withstand the effects of the pollution.

In the same manner, the designer must consider the sound-transmission and
attenuation rating of walls and materials for buildings in high-noise areas, such as
airports, railroads, and highways. The Federal Housing Authority has very specific standards for analyzing sites and exterior walls of senior citizen housing
projects in high-noise areas. In some cases it may be necessary to use the services of an acoustics engineer to determine the type of sound to be filtered and
the type of material to be used. Many exterior cladding systems have been tested
for sound-transmission rating as well as fire rating, and there are methods to cal-
culate the sound-transmission rating similar to the calculation of insulation values.

The mechanical engineer uses the thermal insulating capability and air infiltration limits of the cladding to determine the design of the heating and cooling system. Failure to consult with the mechanical engineer could result in oversized
and inefficient systems, which are more expensive to install and operate. It is
possible that something as minor as a different type of insulation may make a
major difference in the cost and efficiency of the mechanical systems, or at the
other extreme, it may be necessary to select a completely new system or material
to satisfy initial and operating cost restraints.

The selection of the HVAC system can also influence the ability of the cladding to resist water and air infiltration. Many buildings, especially housing projects, are designed with radiant heat and exhaust for toilets and kitchens. Some of these buildings develop high interior negative pressure, which has been found to worsen water leakage problems. A system which creates a higher interior pressure may even help to resist water and air infiltration. However, this could result in lower system efficiency due to loss of air or exfiltration through the same areas through which air would infiltrate under an interior negative-pressure situation.

2 Structural Criteria

Two structural aspects need to be considered when designing cladding for buildings. First, the cladding must be structurally stable when exposed to the effects of wind, earthquakes, and its own weight, and second, the manner in which the cladding system affects the structural system of the building must be analyzed.

Whether the system is designed by the architect (as is common with masonry and stone cladding), the structural engineer (as with cast-in-place concrete), or a manufacturer (as with panel systems or precast concrete, metal, glass, and such), someone must analyze the structural capability of the system to resist the external forces of nature impacting it. Climatological data on wind and seismic zone requirements are given in most codes, and extensive research has been performed to determine their effects on buildings. Many times, however, the use of local building code requirements may not be sufficient for proper design. An example of this would be a 50-m (165-ft) tall building in central New York State. The New York State building code requires that the building be designed to resist a wind load of 1340 Pa (28 psf) acting inward or outward uniformly on its exterior. Research into the manner in which wind affects buildings (see Chapter 3) has shown that the corners and parapets of buildings experience considerably higher outward (negative) pressure than inward (positive) pressure. These facts are taken into account in the American Society of Civil Engineers (1988) publication on wind load design. The same building in central New York State, subjected to the same wind speeds, would be designed for +1300-Pa (+27-psf) and −2700-Pa (−56-psf) loads within 1.2 m (4 ft) of a corner or parapet, +1300 Pa (+27 psf) and −2000 Pa (−42 psf) within 1.2 to 2.4 m (4 to 8 ft) of a corner or parapet and 1300 Pa (27 psf) both positive and negative elsewhere. The detrimental effects of failure to design to resist these loads could be leaks, permanent deflection, or loss of the cladding material.

The cladding system affects the structural system of the building by transmitting the effects of wind or seismic forces to the structure, by assisting the structural system to achieve the necessary stiffness to resist these forces, and by adding weight to the perimeter of the structural frame. The design of the cladding attachment to the structural frame must take into account the ability of the connection to transmit the forces and the location of the connection so that these forces can be absorbed by the structural frame. Some types of cladding systems, such as cast-in-place or precast concrete and masonry, can assist the structural frame in resisting the forces caused by wind and earthquakes. The weight of the cladding system must be considered by the structural engineer in the design of the structural system. The change from a lightweight system, such as glass or metal curtain wall, to precast concrete would have a drastic effect on the structural engineer's design for the building's frame.

3 Cost Criteria

The cost of the cladding is usually a major concern to the owner and architect because of budget constraints. The cost for the exterior walls on a high rise can vary between 5 and 20% of the total construction costs excluding overhead, profit, and design fees. It is important to consider the cost at the earliest stage of design development because once a commitment is made to use a cladding system and material, the only way to reduce costs are to reduce the quality or select a new cladding. In either case, problems are likely to develop. If the quality is reduced, the likelihood of further problems with leaks and material failures is increased. In many cases, when a major design change is made late in the design phase, it does not receive the same amount of detailed analysis by all professionals that the original design received. In addition to these problems, a reduction in quality or change in cladding will result in disappointment to those people who expected something better than what they are receiving.

4 Code Criteria

Most building codes, primarily in larger cities where tall buildings are normally constructed, contain many requirements for the cladding. The most common requirements are criteria for fire ratings, which must be used in the design and met during construction. Fire ratings are usually expressed in terms of hours or flame spread when a fire separation of a given time is not required. These ratings for materials or assemblies are determined by laboratory testing, and the results are published by Underwriters Laboratories, the American Fire Insurance Association, and others.

Another common code requirement relates to structural design for wind loading and seismic resistance. Most major codes contain by reference the requirements of other material codes or association requirements. Examples of these material codes and association requirements are the American Concrete Institute building codes, Aluminum Association guidelines and standards of the American National Standards Institute (ANSI). ANSI, which covers wind loading, normally requires higher wind loads for corners and parapets than building codes. The Aluminum Association guidelines give allowable stresses and design standards for aluminum members and alloys.

Other areas where codes can influence the cladding of the building are zoning codes and local ordinances governing appearance. Some areas, such as suburbs to large cities, include requirements governing the appearance of all buildings built within their jurisdiction. These codes may limit the types of materials which may be used, specify the permitted colors or ranges of colors, or require that the design be approved by a local architectural appearance committee.

A complete code review must be made to determine what basic design and construction criteria are required by the codes or other documents referred to in the code for specific materials, assemblies, or appearances.

5 Esthetic Criteria

As mentioned, the exterior appearance may be preconceived, or the designers may present the owner with alternative choices. The design concept may call for a light and airy appearance utilizing glass or metal curtain walls, or a heavy massive appearance utilizing masonry, concrete, or natural stone. Whether the exterior appearance is selected by the owner or the architect, or chosen to blend in with the site or other buildings, it is important to include the other basic criteria and their respective designers in the process of developing the final design drawings.

6   Erection Criteria

Early in the design phase, the methods of erecting the cladding must be researched and analyzed. The selection of the system and material can be influenced by such factors as methods of lifting, access to or around the building, and on-site or off-site storage capabilities. If the cladding is a single-source system, such as precast concrete or a metal and glass curtain wall, the designer must become familiar with the standard erection procedures in order to identify the problems mentioned, be capable of observing the construction, and participate in construction-phase problem identification and resolution. If the system requires the integration of different suppliers and erectors, such as masonry and stone veneers over a separate back-up system, designers must be more than familiar with erection procedures because they must first specify and detail the interrelationships and then resolve disputes between the different suppliers or erectors during construction.

Each type of material and each manufacturer or supplier of similar materials is likely to have different erection standards or procedures. No attempt will be made here to explain or identify these differences. The following is a discussion of various types of erection procedures which are totally opposite in method of installation. There are many types of erection procedures which utilize the different methods of installation for part of the cladding system. The selection of the procedure for the erection of the cladding must take into account the materials to be used, the type of building and site, work-force availability, contractor experience, and, of course, cost.

The panelized procedure is a method of installation where a single procedure is used to lift and attach a panel to the building, which is complete in terms of exterior finish and support system. Insulation and interior finishes may or may not be included on the panel. The only operations required to complete the exterior enclosure of the building in the area of the panel is to install the joint sealants and clean the exterior. The most obvious example of a panelized cladding procedure is the architectural precast concrete wall panel. The panel is shipped to the job site via truck or, in some cases, cast on the site, lifted off the truck or ground, placed on the building, and bolted or welded to the structural frame. There are many other types of systems using a wide variety of exterior finishes applied to a specially designed back-up system. The most common type of back-up system is the steel-stud or miscellaneous-metal frame. These frames are assembled and covered with the exterior finish in a factory or at the job site and then lifted up to their position on the building. This type of panelization is gaining widespread popularity because of its ability to remain lightweight and the availability of the stud or frame space for insulation.

The design of the cladding panel is heavily influenced by the decision to use the panelized procedure. The panel must be constructed or manufactured with the connections for attaching it to the building and means by which it can be lifted and handled during manufacture, shipment, and erection without interfering with the attachment procedure. The design of the panel must be such that it can resist internal stresses imposed by the lifting and handling. These stresses usually act differently than those which occur while the panel is in place because the attachment connectors are usually in a different location than the lifting points, and the dead-load weight of the panel and not the wind force creates the stresses.

The decision to use the panelized procedure is also influenced by the site and the methods used to construct the building. A crane is normally required to lift the panels into place. The crane type will vary depending on the type of panel, its weight, and the height of the building. For very tall buildings there is usually a tower crane, which was used to erect the superstructure and would be used to erect the panels. In the case of buildings of medium height, a portable crane is often used for erection. It is normally preferred to have an access road around the building so that the panels can merely be lifted vertically into their position. When a panel has to be moved horizontally or around corners, the panel is liable to sway and hit the building or cause other damage to itself or the building. The potential for these problems is reduced when lighter-weight panels are used. However, the lighter-weight panels are more likely to be affected by wind during erection than are heavier panels.

The methods of connecting the panels are other important aspects which must be considered by the designer. The two most common means of attaching panels are bolted connections and welded connections. Bolted connections require attachment members on both the superstructure and the panel. These connections may be steel angles or plates with slotted holes to allow for some adjustment in the field to compensate for field erection tolerances, or an angle or plate on one panel and an attached bolt on the other. This second method allows for only the angle or plate on the one member to have a slotted hole and thus reduces the amount of compensation that can be made during erection. Welded connections are more tolerant of differences due to construction tolerances. The connections are very similar to those used for bolted connections, except that there are no slotted holes and the angles or plates on the panel and the superstructure are welded together. This method is more tolerant because shim plates or extension plates can be added if the plates or angles do not line up perfectly. Most erectors prefer to use the welded connections because they are more forgiving; however, the amount of forgiveness must be controlled. It has not been uncommon for the joint between the vertically stacked architectural precast panels to start out at 19 mm (¾ in.) wide at ground level and grow to 76 mm (3 in.) or more in as few as 15 stories.

The piece-by-piece procedure for erecting cladding is completely opposite from the panelized procedure in that each part of each component is placed on the building individually. Two examples of this procedure are curtain walls and conventional masonry wall. The curtain-wall installation starts with the attachment of the clip angles to the structure, followed by the subgirts, mullions, and finally the installation of the exterior finish panels. Each of the pieces and their associated fasteners and seals are placed individually on the exterior of the building. Normally all of these operations can take place with workers on the individual floor slab or ground. If the individual pieces are heavy or too large to handle on the floor slab, some sort of exterior lifting device is used to position each piece so that it can be connected. In the case of the conventional masonry wall, the first step is to install the back-up (support system) portion of the wall. As discussed, this back-up portion for a masonry wall is usually concrete unit masonry laid one block at a time, with the masonry ties for the brick or light-gauge metal studs installed one stud at a time. The next step in installing the masonry wall normally requires the workers to work from the exterior using scaffolding. When studs are used as the back-up wall, the sheathing, weatherproofing, and brick ties are installed next. In both cases, the steel shelf angles required to support the brick along with the associated flashing are installed. The wall is now ready for the installation of the brick which, like the concrete block back-up wall, is laid one brick at a time. Both types of cladding, curtain wall and brick masonry, are now ready for the installation of the joint sealants and the final cleaning of the exterior finish of the cladding.

The piece-by-piece procedure is more labor intensive at the job site than the panelized procedure, and the quality control is usually not as high as it is in the factory or assembly-line method used to manufacture the cladding for the panelized method. Almost all types of cladding materials, including brick masonry, can be fabricated into panels for installation using the panelized procedure. The experience of the contractor and conventional construction practices with which the local workers are familiar should heavily influence the decision of which method will be used. In many cases it may be advisable for the designer not to make this choice until the contractor is selected, unless site conditions or known experience with one procedure over the other clearly dictates which method should be selected. If the project is being bid competitively, it may be necessary to detail the cladding for both methods and require the contractors to indicate which method they are bidding and to provide proof of experience with that method.

7   Maintenance Criteria

Regular cleaning.   There are three types of maintenance which should be anticipated for the cladding on tall buildings. The first is regular cleaning, which is most common on glass curtain walls. Other types of polished and prefinished cladding materials, such as metal panels and stone, also receive regular cleaning on modern buildings. Many of these buildings have cleaning equipment or supports for cleaning equipment designed into the original building. Many buildings have scaffold supports, called davits, designed into the roof structure. These davits are then used to support scaffolding supplied by firms which specialize in cleaning windows on tall buildings. Older buildings usually had no provision in their design for the support of the window-washing equipment, and scaffolding has to be hung over the roof edge or parapet.

Two problems can develop with these methods of supporting the washing equipment. First, the scaffold used to support the workers who will do the washing is not traveling in a track on the building and is free to move from side to side or outward from the building, creating a safety hazard and the possibility of damaging or marring the exterior cladding. Second, when the scaffold has to be suspended over the roof edge or parapet, it is usually done without proper regard to the stability of the parapet or protection of the roof, roof edge, and parapet.

Buildings such as the Sears Tower and the Standard Oil building in Chicago have motorized scaffold and cleaning equipment which are stored on the roof. When in use, this equipment travels up and down the side of the building on tracks which were designed into the cladding to guide the equipment. Modern technology has made it possible for the cleaning equipment to operate without workers, as wall-washing robots. Not only is it necessary to design the supports and track into the building, but the cleaning agents, as well as the method of applying, scrubbing, and rinsing must be considered to avoid damaging the type of cladding used.

Preventive maintenance.   The second type of maintenance which must be anticipated is known as preventive maintenance. Every building should be inspected on a regular basis to locate and repair minor problems before they become major ones, such as leaks or cladding material falling from the building. The inspection is usually visual and is performed from the ground or an adjacent building, using binoculars or a similar device. If the building has its own washing equipment, it can be used to perform more close-up inspections. If the building does not have its own equipment, scaffold and operators can be rented. All components of the cladding which are visible should be inspected. Sealant joints, masonry joints, seals, and supports for the exterior cladding material are the most likely areas to show signs of wear and deterioration. Regular inspection and repair of minor problems are the most effective safeguards a building owner can take to prevent major problems and expensive repairs in the future. There exist many firms that specialize in building diagnostics and repair. Unfortunately these firms usually are not contacted until a major problem occurs.

Life-cycle replacement.　The third type of maintenance is life-cycle replacement of the cladding material or its accessory components. All materials have a useful life after which it is necessary to replace or repair them. Materials such as masonry or stone have an indefinite life span; however, the mortar and sealant joints around them do not. It is generally felt that properly installed mortar joints should last 30 years before repairs are necessary. Repairs to mortar joints usually consist of removing the exterior 20 mm (¾ in.) of the mortar and placing new mortar in the joints. This process is known as tuck-pointing, and a properly tuck-pointed wall should last approximately 25 years before it is likely to need tuck-pointing again. Most manufactured materials have a manufacturer's warranty or guarantee period. Normally this period can be considered the earliest the material will need to be replaced if it has been installed properly. For most sealants, 10 to 15 years is considered average for a useful life, and most paints and finishes for metals have from 10 to 20 years of useful life. When the paint has become sufficiently faded or unsightly, repainting is necessary. When sealant fails, it must be removed completely and new sealant installed after the joint has been adequately cleaned and primed. Many of the newly developed materials, such as the polymer-based exterior wall insulation and finish systems, are too new to have a known useful life.

1.6 CONDENSED REFERENCES/BIBLIOGRAPHY

1 General

AAMA 1987, *Guide Specifications Manual*

AAMA 1987, *Voluntary Specifications for Aluminum Prime Windows*

ACI 318 1989, *Building Code Requirements for Reinforced Concrete*

ACI 533 1965, *Precast Concrete Wall Panels*

AISI 1980, *Specification for the Design of Cold-Rolled Formed Structural Members*

ANSI A41.1 1953, *American Standard Building Code Requirements for Masonry*

ASTM C270 1989, *Standard Specification for Mortar for Unit Masonry*

ASTM C476 1983, *Standard Specification for Grout for Masonry*

Council on Tall Buildings Group SC 1980, *Tall Building Systems and Concepts*

Masonry Advisory Council 1987, *Design Alerts*

PCI 1977, *Structural Design of Architectural Precast Concrete*

2 Fiber-Reinforced Concrete

ACI 544 1982, *State-of-the-Art Report on Fiber Reinforced Concrete*
Owens-Corning Fiberglas 1986, *Designing with FRC Materials*
PCI SPC-120 1982, *Guide Specification for Glass Fiber Reinforced Concrete Panels*

3 Stucco

Portland Cement Association 1980, *Portland Cement Plaster (Stucco) Manual*
Stucco Manufacturers' Association 1985, *Specifications and Standards for Manufactured*

4 Brick Construction

ACI 530 1988, *Specification for Masonry Structures*
ANSI A41.1 1953, *American Standard Building Code Requirements for Masonry*
ASTM C62 1989, *Building Brick (Solid Masonry Units Made from Clay of Shale)*
ASTM C126 1986, *Ceramic Glazed Structural Clay Facing Tile, Facing Brick, and Solid*
ASTM C216 1989, *Facing Brick (Solid Masonry Units Made from Clay or Shale)*
BIA 1969, *Building Code Requirements for Engineered Brick Masonry*
BIA 1969, *Recommended Practice for Engineered Brick Masonry*
BIA 1987, *Technical Note No. 28B Revised II, Brick Veneer Steel Stud Walls*
BIA-M1 1987, *Standard Specifications for Portland Cement–Lime Mortar for Brick Ma-*

5 Concrete Unit Masonry Construction

ACI 530 1988, *Specification for Masonry Structures*
ANSI A41.1 1953, *American Standard Building Code Requirements for Masonry*
ASTM C55 1985, *Standard Specification for Concrete Building Brick*
ASTM C90 1985, *Standard Specification for Hollow Load-Bearing Concrete Masonry*
ASTM C145 1985, *Standard Specification for Solid Load-Bearing Concrete Masonry Units*
ASTM C270 1989, *Standard Specification for Mortar for Unit Masonry*
ASTM C476 1983, *Standard Specification for Grout for Masonry*

6 Glass Block

American Insurance Association 1976, *National Building Code*
ANSI A41.1 1953, *American Standard Building Code Requirements for Masonry*
BOCA International 1990, *Basic Building Code (Section 1408.0 Structural Glass Block*
ICBO 1988, *Uniform Building Code (Section 2408 Glass Masonry)*
SBCCI 1979, *Standard Building Code (Section 1413 Structural Glass Block)*
UL 1987, *Glass Blocks (120 IW7) HOHT*

7 Stone Materials

ASTM C503 1985, *Marble Building Stone (Exterior)*

ASTM C568 1985, *Limestone Building Stone*
ASTM C615 1985, *Granite Building Stone*
ASTM C616 1985, *Sandstone Building Stone*
ASTM C629 1985, *Slate Building Stone*
Indiana Limestone Institute of America 1984, *Indiana Limestone Handbook*
Marble Institute of America 1989, *Marble Institute of America Manual*
National Building Granite Quarries Association, Inc. 1984, *Specifications for Architectural*
Pennsylvania Slate Producers Guild 1983, *Specification for Exterior Structural Slate*

8 Metal Cladding Materials

AAMA 1987, *Aluminum Curtain Wall Design Manual*
AAMA 1987, *Guide Specifications Manual*
AAMA 1987, *Voluntary Specifications for Aluminum Prime Windows*
NAAMM 1978, *Metal Curtain Wall Manual*

9 Glass

ANSI Z97.1 1987, *Safety Performance Specification and Method of Test for Safety Glazing*
Float Glass Marketing Association 1989, *Glazing Manual*

10 Steel-Stud Support Framing

AISI 1980, *Specification for the Design of Cold Rolled Formed Structural Members*
BIA Tech. Note 28B 1987, *Brick Veneer Steel Stud Walls*

2

Designing Joints and Selecting Sealants

The primary function of a sealant is to keep weather out of the inside of a building through all seasonal and environmental extremes. While sealants average only one-quarter to one-half percent of the entire cost of a building, they are some of the most significant building elements. They must not become too hard and brittle nor too soft and flowable and should have the capability of being installed with a minimum amount of effort and at a low life-cycle cost. Failed sealant can cause many times more damage than its initial cost, and the cost of labor to replace a failed sealant is much greater than the original cost of installation.

Sealants have evolved from the simplest of materials to the high-tech adhesives used today. Historically, sealants were oil-based or resinous-based caulks, which were nothing more than linseed oil and an extending filler. Butyl sealants were introduced in the late 1940s and early 1950s, but were found to have undesirable movement limitations. The first high-performance sealants, introduced in the early 1960s, were based on polysulfide chemistry—the first available cross-linked rubber. These were followed by the silicones and urethanes, which are the products commonly used today in high-rise construction.

2.1 EXPANSION JOINTS

Nearly all sealant joints take up expansion and contraction. The exterior skin of a high-rise building must be designed to expand and contract with daily and annual thermal cycling. Typically, the sealant used to weatherproof the exterior skin of a building must have a movement capacity of at least ±25% of the original joint width. In this situation a low-modulus sealant is desirable.

Modulus is expressed as the ratio of force versus elongation. A low-modulus material takes a relatively low force to give a high elongation, while a high-modulus material takes a high force to give a low elongation. Sealants discussed here include noncuring mastic sealants, high-modulus (up to ±25% movement), medium-modulus (±50%), and low-modulus (+100 to −50%) materials. A low-modulus material takes a low force to stretch. Movement ratings are given in terms of percentage of joint width.

Weatherproofing sealants for external applications should be low-modulus.

31

This will ensure the most forgiving sealant for the application. Many specifiers select medium- or high-modulus sealants because more choices are available to stimulate bidding and occasionally because adhesion characteristics (unprimed to a particular substrate) may be more desirable. More often, the high- and medium-modulus sealants are chosen because the specifier is not aware of the truly low-modulus options and benefits. Buildings of the recent past used some high-modulus sealants because the medium- and low-modulus technology is relatively new.

Sealants with movement ratings lower than ±25% should never be considered for weatherproofing the exteriors of most high-rise buildings. Resealing is so expensive that the extra confidence in products capable of high movement at lower stress on the bond line is a prudent investment.

2.2 DESIGNING NEW JOINTS

Building designers must be aware of the important considerations for joint design: specified live-load movements, specified column shrinkage, thermal movements, construction tolerance, and the types of construction materials to be sealed. Building live-load movements and column shortening must be accounted for in the sealant joints, where movement is contingent on the exterior skin anchorage points. Panels which are to be sealed and only mounted at the column lines must account for specified column shortening, particularly in buildings with concrete structures. If panels or curtain walls are attached to floor slabs, vertical joints between panels attached to these slabs will experience a compression force at the top of the joint and an extension force at the bottom of the joint resulting from live-load deflections.

Many designers fail to recognize that sealants used in weather-seal applications have stress-strain characteristics that will allow a transfer of forces through the joints. Since all sealants have higher moduli of elasticity in cold temperatures, this fact should be noted so that panel anchorages can be sized properly. This is extremely important when designing expansion joints for seismic applications. For practicality of installation, exterior joints should not be sized less than 12.5 mm (½ in.) after tolerances. Smaller joints cannot be cleaned effectively or economically to ensure proper adhesion.

The thermal expansion of the exterior building materials must be calculated by using the temperature differential and the width of the glass panels.

- When using a ±25% sealant, the joint width should be four times the anticipated total movement plus building tolerance.
- When using a ±50% sealant, the joint width should be two times the anticipated movement plus building tolerance.
- When using +100 to −50% sealant, the joint width can be equal to the anticipated movement, but two times the anticipated movement is still optimum.

A joint designed for 100% expansion can only take 50% compression. Thus a joint designed at 100% expansion should be a shear joint, so all movement constitutes an expansion force.

These conservative rules allow the building to be sealed effectively in any season. It is possible for a ±25% sealant to be placed into a joint designed at ±25% and see only movements of −50 to 0% or 0 to +50%, depending on the temperature at installation. If the joint is sealed in midwinter, it could easily see only a −50 to 0% compression cycle. The opposite is true if the joint is sealed in the hottest part of the summer. Thus the equation for joint width advocated by the American Society for Testing and Materials (ASTM C962, 1986) is most appropriate. The equation is

Joint width = 100/movement class × thermal movement + construction

tolerances and other unplanned movements

Construction tolerance cannot be ignored. If expansion joints do not add in this factor, the movement encountered will be a higher percentage of the original joint width. This must be accounted for in all new construction. If a high- or medium-modulus sealant fails because of excessive movement, the only correction available may involve widening the joint—an expensive job that is easier said than done.

Expansion joints must have two-sided adhesion and the joint should look like an hourglass, as shown in Fig. 2.1. This will let the sealant perform like a rubber band. The hourglass configuration gives a large contact on each bonding surface and a smaller area in the center of the joint, thus transferring forces to the bond. Having a width-to-depth ratio of 2:1 is the most "forgiving" configuration for an expansion joint.

Most expansion joints use a foam backer rod behind them to ensure only two-sided adhesions and to limit the thickness of the joint. It is crucial that the backer rod be at least 12.5 to 25% larger than the joint. This snug fit will keep the rod from being forced deeper into the joint as the sealant is applied.

Backer rods are typically polyethylene or polyurethane foam. The polyethylene foams are usually closed-cell and are produced by putting a compressed gas into polyethylene. If punctured, this rod will outgas, causing bubbles to form beneath the sealant at the point of puncture. Instead of being smooth, the joint will look like an overripe string bean. The performance of a silicon sealant will not be affected as long as the bubbles do not blow a hole through it. A more oxidizable sealant such as urethane or polysulfide can eventually develop a hole at this point. Some nonoutgassing polyethylene rods are now emerging.

Polyurethane foam backer rods are usually open-cell and because of their softness and pliability generally require a 25% oversize. Open-cell rods tend to hold water like a sponge while closed-cell backers will let the water drain. This is significant since most exterior weatherproofing sealants will not hold up long under

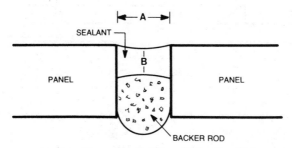

Fig. 2.1   Illustration of width to depth ratio of 2:1.

water. Open-cell rods do have an advantage in that one-part sealants, which air-cure, have an increased cure rate when applied over them.

There are advantages and disadvantages for each type of foam backer rod. Each situation and job must be considered separately. Perhaps the most important fundamental use of the backer rod is to provide backing so that when the sealant is tooled (pushed in the joint), it is also being pushed firmly against the sidewalls. This promotes better wetting and proper adhesion.

2.3 REHABILITATION JOINTS

Thermal cycling and ultraviolet exposure have degraded older sealants much faster than they affect today's sealants. The owner of an older building must face the decision of when to recaulk and what sealant to select. A general rule for rehabilitation work is to use the lowest-modulus sealant available. Daily joint movement should be measured with a scratch tester, as illustrated in Fig. 2.2. A bridge across the joint is mounted on one side of the joint. A pin or screw, which is perpendicular to the bridge, scribes a surface mounted on the other side of the joint. After one full day, the movement can be measured by the scribe marks and interpolated into a fair estimate of the total annual joint movement.

If the joint movement is such that a low-modulus sealant cannot perform in this application, the joint must be effectively widened. This procedure generally involves sawing the joint, but is impractical on metal panels. A band-aid joint may be a possibility, as shown in Fig. 2.3. A bond breaker is applied over the old sealant and onto the exterior face of the building. The sealant is then applied over the bond breaker tape and at least 6.35 mm (¼ in.) past the bond breaker onto the exterior surface. This has then effectively widened the joint. If a simple reinstallation is the answer to the rehabilitation job, it will require a complete removal of the old sealant. Labor for removal and prepping is a major expense in a rehabilitation project.

Calculating joint movement in shear is easier than many envision. When a joint moves 90° in shear, the extension follows the hypotenuse of a right triangle. Figure 2.4 shows a 25-mm (1-in.) wide joint which has moved 25 mm (1 in.) in perpendicular shear. If one examines the distance between the two joint faces at

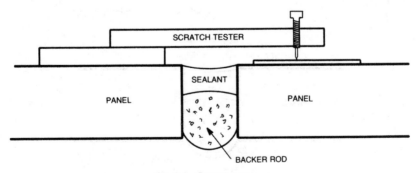

Fig. 2.2 Scratch tester.

points A and B, it is found that this is only a 41% joint movement. The distance between B_1 and B_2 is 25 mm (1 in.). By the pythagorean theorem,

$$(AB_1)^2 + (B_1B_2)^2 = (AB)^2 \tag{2.1}$$

When solving for AB_2 it is determined that $AB_2 = 35.92$ mm (1.414 in.). Solving for the joint extension, we find that the joint has extended 41%.

This same calculation is used for longitudinal shear. The West Coast of the United States has seismic activity which warrants that buildings must be able to withstand shear movement of about 38 mm (1.5 in.) at every floor. Joints designed for seismic conditions should use low-modulus sealants. A 100% class sealant permits the narrowest joint, but special care is required in the calculations to ensure that 100% movement is all that is expected. The construction tolerances must be considered.

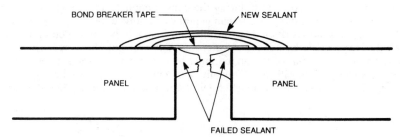

Fig. 2.3 Band-aid joint.

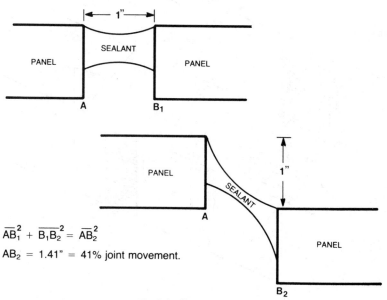

$\overline{AB_1}^2 + \overline{B_1B_2}^2 = \overline{AB_2}^2$

$AB_2 = 1.41" = 41\%$ joint movement.

Fig. 2.4 Shear movement.

2.4   SPLICE JOINTS

Some glazing systems between stone or metal spandrel panels have the glass set into an aluminum can (at the head and sill). Gaskets hold the glass snugly into place between the cans (Fig. 2.5). The head and sill cans cannot run the length of a building and must be spliced. Most often only the sill can is spliced because it must hold water and drain the water out through weep holes. These splices occur every 3 to 4.5 m (10 to 15 ft) and undergo a substantial amount of thermal movement. At every splice a piece of metal is inserted into the two cans and anchored to one side with a rivet or set in a bed of curing sealant. The other side has a thin splice of metal sliding into it. In the past, both sides of the splice were imbedded in a noncuring mastic sealant commonly known as curtain-wall sealant. The joint between splice and sill is only about 0.635 mm (0.025 in.), so any significant movement results in several hundred percent extension, which is substantially beyond the performance capabilities of the curing sealant.

If a problem is encountered during the construction of a building with a conventional splice joint, the problem can generally be solved by using a curing sealant. When the splice is riveted to one sill can, it should be imbedded in a curing sealant. This acts as an adhesive water seal and will not shear because of the rivet. The opposite end of the splice must have a bond breaker applied equally over the splice and the sill can. Typically, a 25-mm (1-in.) tape can be used to put 12.5 mm (½ in.) on the splice and 12.5 mm (½ in.) on the sill can. Then the curing

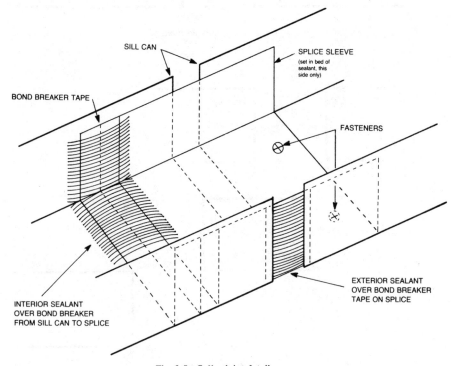

Fig. 2.5   Splice joint detail.

sealant is applied over the bond breaker tape and onto the splice and sill can—a band-aid joint (see Fig. 2.3).

The small joint on the exterior of a splice is one of the hardest joints to seal on any building. Before the splice is set down, a bond breaker must be applied to the splice sleeve so that the exterior joint can be sealed between the two sill cans. This joint typically is 1.6 by 12.5 mm ($\frac{1}{16}$ by $\frac{1}{2}$ in.) and will very easily see ±50% joint movement.

Denver, Colorado, has the most extreme thermal movements in the spring and fall of the year. A 12.5-mm ($\frac{1}{2}$-in.) exterior joint will see a full 6.35 mm ($\frac{1}{4}$ in.) of movement in 3.6 m (12 ft) of aluminum sill can. Some joints will see 0 to ±50% depending on the time of day they are sealed. When excessive thermal movement takes place during a sealant's cure cycle, the joint could become rippled and bumpy. There is no way to prevent this in extreme thermal cycles. The sealant may lose adhesion to the sill can edges during this thermal cycling. One-part sealants cure from the outside in and adhesion is the last property to develop. If this happens, the sill can edges should have an adhesion promoter or primer applied to them before sealant application. If the phenomenon still exists, a lower-modulus sealant should be used. As a final solution, the joints will have to be widened or a band-aid joint applied.

2.5 TYPES OF SEALANTS USED IN HIGH-RISE CONSTRUCTION

One of the most important points in joint design or sealant selection is choosing a sealant that has the needed movement ability. Be sure the movement ability being quoted has been tested by the ASTM C719 test method (1986). These test data are best quoted when tests are conducted by an independent lab. It is the test method used in federal standards and ASTM standards.

The two-part and one-part polysulfides were some of the first high-performance construction sealants. They have relatively high modulus characteristics with joint movement ratings of ±12.5 to ±25% in ASTM C719. The one-part polysulfides have an extremely long cure rate related to the moisture vapor transmission rate of the cured rubber. The two-part sealants have a moderate cure rate, curing in a matter of a day. The two part sealants also have a wide variety of colors available. Polysulfides have a service temperature range of −29 to 82°C (−20 to 180°F), have good abrasion resistance, and are used somewhat in swimming pools and aqueducts. Before the application of these sealants, surfaces must be clean and dry. The two-part sealants are very popular in the insulating glass market because of their relatively low moisture vapor transmission rate, cost, and quick cure.

The principal mode of failure in a polysulfide is with a compression set that gets progressively worse over the years. Another caution is that these generally require a primer on concrete and similar materials, and often these primers are omitted. Diligence to ensure the application of primers is fundamental to success. Few can stand water immersion for prolonged periods and still accommodate any movement.

The one-part and two-part urethanes are known for their abrasion resistance or toughness. Their service temperature ranges are advertised as low as −45.5°C (−50°F), but their upper limits are still at 82°C (180°F). A note of caution is that they are quite stiff in the very cold. These sealants are mostly high-modulus materials, but some of them fall into a medium-modulus category with movements up to ±50%. These materials are paintable and are desirable on smaller concrete structures where the paint scheme can change with every building owner. They must be applied to clean dry surfaces. The one-part sealants cure rather slowly, but the two-part, mixed on site, cure in a day or two. The primary shortcoming of urethanes is their continued curing, which results in the sealant getting harder and harder and eventually losing the ability to perform at the specified movement range.

The two-part modified urethanes are good general caulking materials. They have acceptable weatherability and excellent abrasion resistance, as described. These sealants are not quick to cure and may take a few days to vulcanize. The urethanes, polysulfides, and modified urethanes all have good weatherability, but they chalk, crack, and craze from the ultraviolet energy emitted from the sun. The joints always look clean and dry because the joints are constantly degrading and chalking. Eventually these sealants wear away, although some are considered better because the initial cure is more complete and there is less or slower hardening with time than with many typical urethanes.

Noncuring sealants have found a niche with the splice joints mentioned earlier. They have also been used on screw heads and end dams in curtain-wall construction. These applications are mainly to keep water from leaking into the building. They are permanently sticky and are never used in visible joints.

Silicones are the last sealants covered here. Silicones are unique in that ultraviolet light and thermal cycling do not break down the sealant in any way. They stay rubbery and flexible throughout their life. When put into a weatherometer, the silicones do not become brittle, chalk, or crack. They have all modulus bases covered, from ±12.5 to +100 to 50%, with one- and two-part sealants. The moisture vapor transmission rate for silicones is relatively high, resulting in a quick cure rate. Silicone sealants have polymers made up of silicon-to-oxygen chains, whereas the other types of sealants are made up of organic chains.

The stability of the silicon-to-oxygen bond is greater than that of typical carbon-to-carbon or carbon-to-oxygen bonds. The silicon-to-oxygen bonds do not absorb energy in the ultraviolet wavelength. Consequently the ultraviolet wavelength from the sun will not affect the silicon-to-oxygen bonds. Silicones are unsurpassed for weatherability. This high internal bond energy also gives wider service temperature ranges, from −51 to 232°C (−60 to 450°F), depending on the chemistry used to cross-link the silicone sealants. Antifungal agents can be incorporated into the sealants, making them an excellent bathtub caulk.

Two-part silicones have been introduced into the market because they have variable, quick cure rates. Some applications involve insulating glass sealants or structural glazing of unitized curtain-wall systems.

In addition to normal weatherseals and expansion joints, silicones are used in glazing. In glazing details where the sun can shine on the sealant, almost nothing else is recommended. Silicones do not have good abrasion resistance, however. They are "pickable" and should not be used in areas such as a door perimeter in a school.

Silicones are generally not paintable. When a silicone joint moves, any paint on the surface will crack and fall to the ground. All the other sealants mentioned are available in a variety of colors. Some silicones are also available in clear. The chief attributes of silicones are their consistent performance and 20-year life expectancy. Their chief disadvantage is that they will often get dusty and must be cleaned.

Caulking materials do not exist which consider themselves "siliconized."

These are generally interior and consumer sealants that use a silicone fluid as a plasticizer so that the materials extrude from the caulking cartridge more easily. They may have a bit of silica filler to control slump, or a bit of silane to aid adhesion. In no way do these systems mimic the performance of a true silicone sealant.

2.6 JOINT PREPARATIONS

All sealants mentioned here must have clean and dry surfaces before adhesion can be expected to develop. The best way to prepare surfaces is to use the two-rag solvent wipe. This involves two clean lint-free rags—one rag soaked with an organic solvent such as MEK, xylene, or toluene and a second rag that is dry. The solvent-soaked rag is used to soak the surface to be sealed. The dry rag is used to wipe the residual solvent before it evaporates. Using a paintbrush to apply the solvent and letting the solvent evaporate is not acceptable.

Most sealants have primers or adhesion enhancers. The latter are applied to surfaces that are difficult to adhere to. The primers must be applied to surfaces which have already been cleaned. Cleaning is not priming, and vice versa.

2.7 BOND BREAKERS

Some of the most effective bond breakers are the foam backer rods discussed earlier. There are also several others. Bond breaker tapes are the most popular for applications where foam rods are not practical. Polyethylene tape is the most commonly used tape, although some sealant will even adhere to this. Teflon tape is also available. Paraffin wax can be used as a bond breaker. It is convenient because it can be drawn on, but it is also dangerous since it can contaminate surfaces. Butyl glazing tape in 3.2- or 1.6-mm (⅛- or ¹⁄₁₆-in.) thickness is a good bond breaker. It can be cut and forced in place with finger pressure. Polyethylene tapes do not adhere well to cold metal surfaces, but butyl tapes have enough tack that cold weather is not a problem. These are used in weather seals where two-sided adhesion is desirable.

2.8 SEALANT INSTALLATIONS

When applying sealant it is important that it be pushed into the joint with the caulking gun. This means that a very small mound of sealant should always be in front of the nozzle as it moves along the joint. This will let the installer know how the sealant is flowing into the joint. Joints are to be void-free, and this technique pushes the air out of the joint. Any nonsag sealant should always be pushed and never pulled.

All sealants must be tooled off after application and before a skin forms on the exterior bead. When tooling, the joint should be struck down once with a dry tool, ensuring that extra force is applied to wet out the entire surface to be sealed. Many caulkers use a tooling solution of soap and water. If the joint is underfilled and the soap solution gets between the surface and the sealant, adhesion will not develop. A break in the sealant bond under these circumstances can rarely be found. A caulker soon learns that the more a joint is tooled, the worse it looks. Tooling once is necessary, twice is excessive. Tooling aids such as soap solutions are rarely recommended.

After the joints have been cleaned and before the sealant is installed it may be necessary to mask the joint with tape. The tape must be removed after tooling and before a good skin has formed. Some silicones cure quite quickly and tape removal must be done within a few minutes after sealant application.

2.9   FIELD ADHESION PROCEDURE

All sealants should be checked and documented for adhesion after installation of the first part of any job. With all of the hours which go into design, cleaning, installation, and cleanup, the sealant must perform the way it is supposed to. Documented field adhesion testing should be a part of every job file. High- and medium-modulus sealants when used in structural glazing must show a cohesive failure to the substrates when they are pulled out of the joint; this means the bond is stronger than the sealant itself.

Low-modulus sealants and sealants used to weather-seal, the most typical application, should maintain a constant bond line when the sealant is extended to two times its joint movement rating while being pulled perpendicular to the joint. This is accomplished by cutting out a 50-mm (2-in.) tab of the sealant, as shown in Fig. 2.6. Grab the tab at the 25-mm (1-in.) mark on the sealant and pull per-

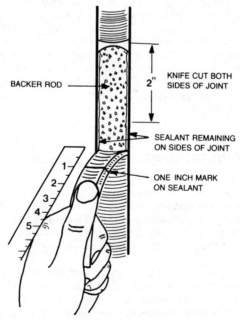

BACKER ROD

KNIFE CUT BOTH
SIDES OF JOINT

2"

SEALANT REMAINING
ON SIDES OF JOINT

ONE INCH MARK
ON SEALANT

Fig. 2.6   Low-modulus field adhesion test.

pendicular to the joint or to the 37-mm (1.5-in.) mark on the ruler for a sealant rated at ±25% movement, to the 50-mm (2-in.) mark for a sealant rated at ±50% movement, and to the 76-mm (3-in.) mark for a sealant rated at 100% movement. When pulling this tape, the bond line should not move. This should be wet (immersed if possible) and rechecked after 7 days' immersion. (Some manufacturers accept 1-day water immersion as a significant field test.)

2.10 STRUCTUAL GLAZING

This area is unique to silicones. Structural glazing sealants must be used as adhesives, and the rules of joint design discussed earlier do not always apply. The goals of a structural glazing sealant must be long life, sufficient adhesive strength to hold the glass or panel under wind loading, and a seal which will absorb the thermal movement differential between glass or panels and frames.

Silicone is defined as structural when it is used to transfer loads averted on glass or panels to frames which are attached to a building mechanically. Structural silicone adheres glass, metal panels, stone panels, or tiles to metal frames. Figure 2.7 shows a typical design for structural silicone with the key points illustrated. The glue thickness must never be less than 6.4 mm (¼ in.). This will ensure that the glazier can fill the joint with the adhesive sealant material.

The glue thickness dimension also takes up the thermal movement differential between the glass and metal. The maximum thermal movement differential allowable for this sealant to absorb is a 15% joint extension. This is figured at the worst case, that is, largest panel under largest thermal cycle, and using the shear movement calculation discussed earlier. As a general rule, the 6.4-mm (¼-in.) glue thickness will accommodate glass up to 2.4 m (8 ft), 8 mm (5/16 in.) will accommodate glass up to 3 m (10 ft) tall, and 9.5 mm (3/8 in.) will accommodate glass up to 3.6 m (12 ft) tall. This assumes that the metal frames are aluminum under a 71°C (160°F) thermal cycle. When structural glazing in Alaska, more glue thickness of sealant will be required because of the higher thermal cycle.

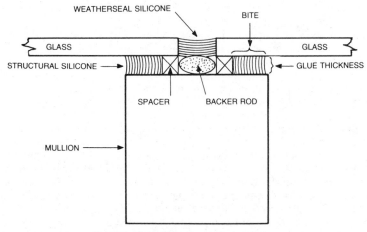

Fig. 2.7 Typical structural glazing design.

The bite, or the amount of glass gripped by the frame, is determined by the equation derived from the theory of trapezoidal loading on glass. It is equal to one-half the smallest dimension of the largest lite multiplied by the wind load and divided by the design strength of the sealant. In U.S. customary units, the equation and proper conversion factors can be expressed as follows:

$$\text{Bite (in.)} = \frac{0.5 \times \text{smallest dimension of largest lite (ft)} \times \text{windload (lb/ft}^2)}{\text{design strength (20 psi} \times 12 \text{ in/ft)}} \quad (2.2)$$

What kind of sealant is a structural sealant? A structural sealant may be considered medium- or high-modulus. It must see its design strength of 138, 103, or 83 kPa (20, 15, or 12 psi) at about 15% extension and must have at least a 2.5:1 safety factor. The maximum industry standard design strength in general use is 138 kPa (20 psi). A structural sealant must exhibit at least the design force of 138 kPa (20 psi) to keep the glass edge from being pulled off the setting block when pulled to 3.2 mm (⅛ in.). The force at break is at least 345 kPa (50 psi) in standard joint design. All silicones used today for structural glazing do show a safety factor greater than 2.5:1. This number was chosen initially because the factors of safety of glass and metal in structural glazing designs are not greater than 2.5:1.

When sizing joints using Eq. 2.2 it is important to round up the joint to the next 1.6 mm (1/16 in.). This avoids putting more than design strength on the sealant with wind loading. Experienced designers will put the design force on the structural sealant at 138 or 103 kPa (15 or 12 psi). This is not because there are plans to use a weaker sealant, but because such designs put less stress on the bond line, the primary area of concern in structural glazing. Testing for adhesion to actual job materials with the silicone sealant is required on all structural glazing jobs. The sealant manufacturer tests the materials before the job begins and makes recommendations regarding those tests. The actual job site materials are tested on the job site, with the surface prepared by the workers who will perform the entire operation. The industry standard test done by the manufacturer is a peel adhesion test according to ASTM C794 (1990), which includes an adhesion evaluation after 7 days of water immersion. Some sealants require primers to adhere to certain aluminum finishes or paints. It is crucial that all adhesion testing be performed before job start-up. The field adhesion test is the same as the field test noted earlier, but the tab is pulled until it breaks. The tab must break before losing adhesion or the job cannot proceed.

Compatibility of the sealant with the materials it contacts also needs to be determined. It has been found that some gasket types will bleed fluids and oils into silicone sealants and cause adhesion failure. Glass, metal, tile, or stone do not bleed anything into the sealants and are checked for adhesion only. Gaskets, spacers, and setting blocks which contact the structural sealant must again be tested for compatibility before job start-up.

The industry standard test for compatibility involves putting a gasket or spacer material on a piece of glass and extruding a light- and dark-colored silicone sealant onto the gasket with the sealant adhering to glass (Fig. 2.8). The sample is then subjected to ultraviolet light at 2000 to 4000 μW/cm^2 at 50°C (122°F) for 21 days. After the sample is removed from the ultraviolet chamber, it is checked for sealant discoloration, sealant adhesion to the gasket, and sealant adhesion to glass. Most neoprene, ethylyne propylene diene monomer (EPDM), and some PVC gaskets will cause the sealants to discolor in this test. This discoloration is caused by the oils and plasticizers in the gaskets migrating through the silicone and oxidizing on the sealant surface. Sometimes the sealant will lose adhesion to the glass, but this only happens when severe discoloration is noted and migration is excessive. The adhesion of sealant to the gasket is also checked.

The only materials that should come in full contact with structural silicone are materials that do not discolor white sealants after the 21-day ultraviolet exposure. The materials which are most often compatible with structural silicone are urethane and polyethylene foams, some PVC gaskets, and silicone gaskets. Gaskets which show a slight discoloration on light-colored sealant and no discoloration on dark-colored sealant can be used at incidental contact points touching the structural sealant.

Many architectural specifications require letters from the sealant manufacturer stating adhesion and compatibility test results, instructions on the proper installation of the sealant, and an approval of the structural sealant design before caulking can begin. This method eliminates many problems because the sealant manufacturer can alert the contractor to problem areas or state disapproval of some of the system components and have the architect require the contractor to change the system. The sealant manufacturers are promoting quality by offering their testing facilities and making recommendations based on their past experience.

The most common structural glazing system today is two-sided structural glazing. This is very popular for getting the ribbon window effect. The head and sill of a piece of glass are set in a can (or frame) and are simply held with gaskets. The back of the glass along the verticals is structurally glazed to a metal mullion where the two pieces of glass meet (Fig. 2.9).

Another common type of system is one-sided structural glazing. This usually occurs in a building with punched openings for windows. Figure 2.10 shows a punch opening window with two pieces of glass. A metal mullion runs behind the glass in the center and has the same design as that shown in Fig. 2.9. The other three sides of this glass are held in the punched opening mechanically with gaskets.

Four-sided structural glazing is another common practice. This system uses silicone on all four sides of the glass to adhere its back side to the metal frame (Fig. 2.11). The equations for calculating bite and glue thickness discussed earlier also apply here.

One more consideration is dead-load shear on the sealant. Figure 2.11 shows a horizontal member with a fin and setting block under the insulated glass unit. Insulating glass manufacturers will not allow their units to be used in a finless glazing system because the outboard lite of the unit would be hanging on only the insulating glass sealant. Figure 2.12 shows a finless glazing system. Finless glazing can only be done with monolithic glass or panels.

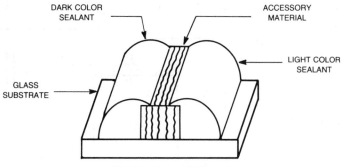

DARK COLOR
SEALANT

ACCESSORY
MATERIAL

LIGHT COLOR
SEALANT

GLASS
SUBSTRATE

Fig. 2.8 Compatibility test.

The most important aspect in finless structural glazing is that the sealant must not see more than 6.895 kPa (1 psi) in dead-load shear. The 6.895 kPa (1 psi) is simply the weight of the glass or panel divided by the contact area of the silicone around the perimeter. Many designers use 3.45 kPa (0.5 psi) or less as maximum dead load. This is conservative but very acceptable.

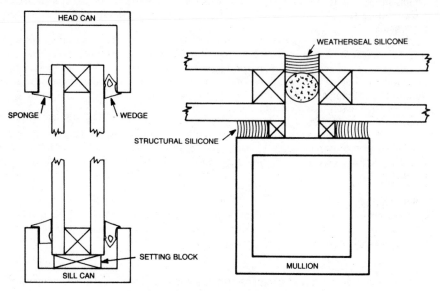

Fig. 2.9 **Two-sided structurally glazed insulating glass.**

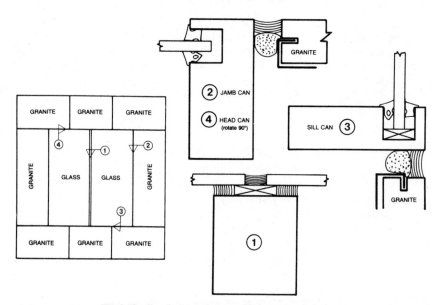

Fig. 2.10 **Punched-opening one-sided structural glazing.**

The Cygnus panel system uses this concept of finless structural glazing. In this system, structural silicone adheres tiles or stone panels to galvanized metal decking. The wind load on a 0.3- by 0.3-mm (1- by 1-ft) tile is not merely a consideration when compared to the 6.895-kPa (1-psi) maximum dead-load shear. This panel system can be considered a unitized structural siliconed system. Unitized

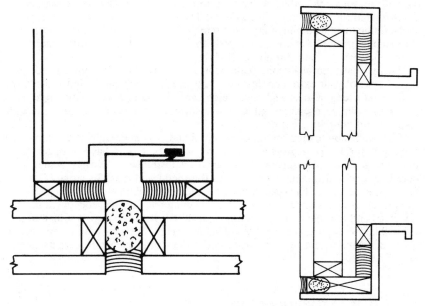

Fig. 2.11 Four-sided structural glazing with insulating glass.

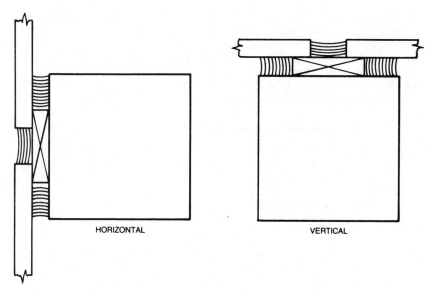

Fig. 2.12 Four-sided structural glass with monolithic glass and no dead-load support.

systems are constructed in a shop, transported to the job site, and hung onto the building. Much more quality control can be exercised on the surface preparation and installation on the structural silicone sealant. Field glazing is not considered bad, but this system offers more quality control. The structural sealant is shop-applied in an L-shaped bead, as illustrated in Fig. 2.13.

The sealant must be applied from the top down because caulkers cannot reasonably get under the tables to caulk from the underside. Oversized glass can be disastrous in the unitized glazing system. The dimension between glass edge and metal frame must be a minimum of 6.4 mm (¼ in.). If this dimension is decreased, the silicone cannot be applied effectively to the back of the joint. Structural joints cannot perform to their full potential if they are not filled.

Two-part structural silicone sealants have found a niche in unitized shop glazing because of their extremely fast cure and excellent adhesion. Unitized systems of the past used one-part sealants, which can take up to 3 weeks to cure in large joints. The two-part sealants will cure to a soft rubber in about 3 hours and can be shipped and hung the next day.

Field adhesion testing should be required and documented by the architect for each structural glazed project. Structural sealants should have stronger bonds than the sealants themselves. This can be determined by cutting some of the cured sealant and pulling it away from the metal and glass or stone. Cohesive failure should result. The sealant must rip and not exhibit any adhesion loss to the substrates. If adhesion loss does occur, cleaning and sealing procedures must be reviewed and the sealant manufacturer consulted. Reputable sealant manufacturers will know about problems that constantly plague their customers, and can offer on-site service and support, an essential element in successful structural glazing.

2.11 INSULATING GLASS SEALANT

The two most common types of insulating glass sealants are two-part polysulfides and two-part silicone sealants. One-part butyl and one-part silicones are also used, and some two-part modified polyurethanes have entered the market. The two-part polysulfide is used primarily in the residential market, but is losing the market share of commercial work to two-part silicones. Insulating glass units must have a silicone seal as the secondary seal before they can be used in structural glazing applications. Two-part silicone insulating glass sealants are sensitive

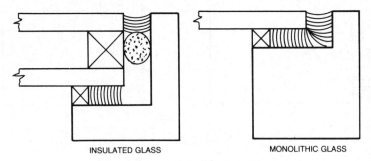

INSULATED GLASS   MONOLITHIC GLASS

Fig. 2.13 Typical structural silicone joint for unitized curtain wall.

to the acid cure of one-part silicones. Acetic acid given off during the vulcanization of the acid cure silicones has been found to diminish the adhesion properties of the insulating glass sealant. These designs are not approved by any insulating glass manufacturers.

Insulating glass sealants bond two pieces of glass separated by a metal spacer filled with a desiccant (Fig. 2.14). Some polysulfide units and all silicone units have a dual seal. The polysulfides have a low moisture vapor transmission. The moisture barrier used in these units is polyisobutylene, a noncuring mastic sealant which is not drastically affected by ultraviolet rays.

2.12 FIRE-STOP SEALANTS

Fire-stop sealants must pass a back-side temperature rise minimum, a constant flame up against them, and a high-pressure hose stream test. Cementitious grouts and putties can easily pass these tests, but they leak smoke and gasses. Recently the introduction of silicone two-part foams, one-part silicones, and one-part chlorinated hydrocarbon sealants have been able to pass 2- and 3-hour fire ratings. The joints must be properly designed to the appropriate specifications (Underwriters Laboratories in the United States of America, for example). The use of curing sealants will help ensure that deadly smoke will not pass through the penetrations. One product currently on the market is an intumescent grout material. When exposed to flame, it will swell and form a tight seal. Unfortunately, before

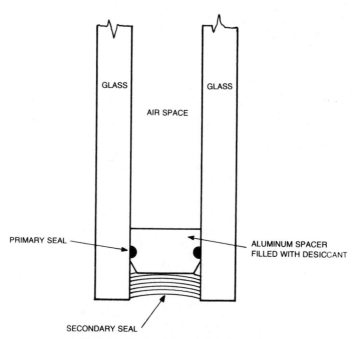

GLASS

GLASS

AIR SPACE

PRIMARY SEAL

ALUMINUM SPACER
FILLED WITH DESICCANT

SECONDARY SEAL

Fig. 2.14   Dual-sealed insulating glass unit.

it heats to the activation temperature, smoke will pass through the penetrations and possibly endanger lives. A fire, gas, and smoke seal is desirable.

2.13 CONDENSED REFERENCES/BIBLIOGRAPHY

ASTM C719 1986, *Test Method for Adhesion and Cohesion of Elastomeric Joint Sealants*
ASTM C962 1986, *Guide for Use of Elastomeric Joint Sealants*
ASTM C794 1990, *Test Method for Adhesion-in-Peel of Elastomeric Joint Sealants*

3

Design Issues for Wind Loads

3.1 THE NATURE OF WIND LOADS

The cladding or exterior surface of any building must resist thousands of cycles of wind loading every day. During storms it is buffeted by gusts from various directions, and over a long period of time the building structure and the external cladding must continue to accept these forces without losing strength or weather-resisting qualities. For specific information on wind, readers are directed to the chapter on wind loading and wind effects in volume CL of the Monograph on Planning and Design of Tall Buildings (Council on Tall Buildings, Group CL, 1980).

The wind, as it strikes the building, is affected by the climatic conditions for the geographical area, the surrounding terrain, and the effects of other buildings adjacent to the site. This terrain starts working on the wind several miles upwind from the building site and creates a wind profile, which describes the shape and gradient of the wind, including turbulence, eddies, and such, in the boundary layer. This is a layer of air occurring sometimes several thousand feet above the ground, separating laminar flow from uniform flow. All air above the boundary layer is moving in uniform flow, and is unaffected by the roughness or character of the ground surface terrain. Air below the boundary layer is in laminar flow and contains turbulence, gusts, and eddies. Laminar flow increases with altitude as it approaches the boundary layer.

Wind loadings can be analyzed as statistical variations, which will include events that can be expected over a period of time. This means the design load must anticipate a statistical recurrence of an event over a 50- or 100-year period, which may represent the life of the building. The likelihood of a wind or storm event occurring can be interpreted from recorded meteorological data of the local area. Possibility and chance are inherent in any design for expected maximum wind loads derived from recent advances in fluid dynamics. To study these events, the art of wind tunnel testing has been applied successfully to building design during the last two decades. By assuming a 50- or 100-year recurrence interval of peak statistical wind loads, one can expect a reasonable design factor, as compared to a 10,000-year occurrence interval, which would amount to a cataclysmic event. In places like Hong Kong, Houston, Miami, and New York, major storms and their recurrence intervals have been studied in detail to establish critical wind patterns. Figure 3.1 shows a schematic section of a hurricane or typhoon taken from such data. It is uneconomical to build or design for events beyond a certain probability.

A significant characteristic of modern building design is lighter cladding and more flexible frames. These features produce an increased vulnerability of glass and cladding to wind damage and result in larger deflections of the building frame. In addition, an increased use of pedestrian plazas at the base of buildings has brought about a need to consider the effects of wind and gustiness in the design of these areas.

The building geometry itself may increase or decrease wind loading on the structure. Wind forces may be modified by nearby structures, which can produce beneficial shielding or adverse increases in loading. Overestimating loads results in uneconomical design; underestimating may result in cladding or window failures. Tall structures have historically produced unpleasant wind and turbulence conditions at their bases. The intensity and the frequency of objectionable winds in pedestrian areas are influenced both by the shape of the structure itself and by the shape and position of adjacent building structures.

3.2 MODELING AND TESTING

Techniques for wind tunnel modeling of proposed structures have been developed and allow the prediction of wind pressures on cladding and windows, overall structural loading, and wind velocities and gusts in pedestrian areas adjacent to the building. Information on sidewalk-level gustiness allows plaza areas to be protected by design changes before the building is constructed. Accurate knowledge of the intensity and distribution of the pressures on the structure permits an adequate but economical selection of cladding strength to meet selected maximum design winds and overall wind loads when designing the frame for flexure control.

Two kinds of testing are used to examine the effects of wind on the design. The first is a wind tunnel test on a small-scale model of the project and its envi-

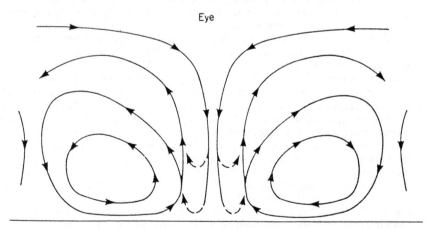

Eye

Fig. 3.1 Schematic section through a typhoon.

ronment. The second is testing full-scale portions of the building facade to measure the actual performance of the curtain-wall or cladding system, which is usually done at a full-scale curtain-wall testing establishment.

To determine external wind pressures for the design of cladding, there are also essentially two approaches. Either the values given by the appropriate code of practice or building regulations are used, or wind tunnel testing is employed. The latter is indulged in for a variety of complex reasons. Quite often clients and architects (and, indeed, engineers too) go down this route in the belief that they are going to obtain design values which are in some way "better."

Unfortunately there are a variety of different ways in which tests can be carried out. Most good wind tunnel establishments will attempt to simulate the atmospheric boundary layer, but some still carry out wind tests using uniform flow, which will normally produce results that are totally irrelevant to cladding design.

A scale model is placed in a wind tunnel to determine design loads for cladding. The model is built to include between 200 and 600 pressure taps at various locations. These pressure taps are in turn connected to transducers which convert pressure to electrical signals that are fed into a computer. In this way, continuous readings can be obtained from all the pressure taps over a given time span, and these can be integrated to read peak wind pressures as the wind comes from various directions.

In the boundary-layer wind tunnel the wind is modeled to simulate the actual speed and turbulence to be encountered at the building site. This is done by approximating the roughness and terrain profiles affecting the wind as it approaches the building site. The model is rotated on a turntable to simulate wind from all directions. The wind above a certain height flows smoothly and is unaffected by the terrain of the ground below. The layer of air between the ground and the point where the wind flows smoothly (usually several thousand feet above the ground) is called the boundary layer and is subject to laminar flow. This layer of air contains the many whirlpools, eddies, and turbulent flows that shape the wind that hits the building. Figures 3.2 and 3.3 show the wind profiles to be simulated in the wind tunnel.

For the structural design of building frames, another sort of wind tunnel test model is sometimes used to study the dynamic qualities of the building as affected by the wind. This is called a dynamic wind pressure test, and it uses another type of model that reflects the stiffness and motion characteristics of the structure. Instead of pressure taps, this model is designed to measure movements and dynamic properties of a building in the wind, which includes deformation, twisting, and oscillations. For a large high-rise project, both types of wind tunnel tests are very useful.

The most rigorous approach to testing is that developed and used by Professor Alan Davenport at the Boundary Layer Wind Tunnel Laboratory (University of Western Ontario, Canada). Results from the wind tunnel tests are integrated with the wind climate probability distribution by direction in order to produce external pressures having a specified probability of exceedance, at each point on the building surface. Unfortunately the necessary wind climate data are not always available.

3.3 WIND SIMULATION

To model the appropriate wind conditions in the wind tunnel, a mean wind velocity having the desired probability of occurrence must first be determined. This must be established from local meteorological records. The correct variation in velocity with height and mixture of gusts must also be simulated from a statistical analysis of the local wind data (Figs. 3.3, 3.4, and 3.5.)

Just as a length scale can be used for the model, a time scale is also used; for example, 1:100. Thus a 10-sec gust acting on the real structure would be equivalent to 0.1 sec in the wind tunnel. As the readings have to be interpreted statistically to deal with gusts and continuously fluctuating velocities, this compressed time scale will enable sufficiently large samples of data to be obtained within an acceptable length of time. Figure 3.6 shows a pressure trace for one location in a typical wind tunnel test, with the wind coming from one direction (in this case 45°).

The readings taken from the pressure taps and transducers on the model consist of electrical signals which are introduced into the computer. The results (from all directions) are recorded, integrated, and printed out by the computer to show peak pressures for each and every pressure tap as well as maximum gust pressures during gusts of different durations (1 sec, 3 sec, 10 sec, 1 min, and so on). Mean values, which are useful in establishing design loadings, will include the 3-sec, 10-sec, and 1-min gusts and mean hourly wind speed. From the computer printout, contour plots are made for each facade of the building, showing the maximum positive and negative wind pressures to be expected (see Section 3.8 and Figs. 3.15 and 3.16).

Since readings from wind tunnel tests are expressed as dimensionless coefficients, these are multiplied by a factor derived from the dimensions of the wind tunnel and model, and from recorded weather data, describing mean hourly wind speeds near the site. This procedure is used to arrive at full-scale pressures to be expected on the actual building. To get the design pressures, a factor is added to compensate for predictability and statistical variation.

Peak gust pressures and their frequency of recurrence have been found statis-

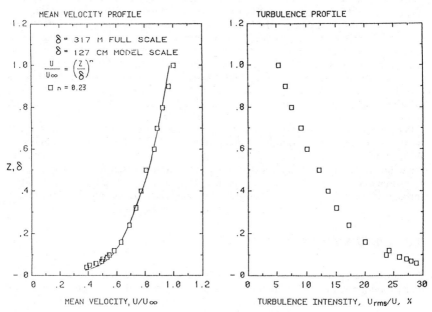

Fig. 3.2 Mean velocity and turbulence profiles approaching the model.

tically to conform with certain distribution curves such as the gaussian distribution for fluctuating surface pressure about an hourly mean (see Section 3.5 and Fig. 3.11), or the Fisher-Tippett type 1 distribution for occurrences of mean hourly wind speeds from storms over a period of time (see Section 3.5 and Fig. 3.13). The prediction of extreme values is still a matter of differing opinions among experts. Statistical and mathematical interpretations of this problem have been explored in depth in studies at the University of Bristol, United Kingdom, and at Colorado State University, United States, among others. Besides wind tunnel tests, full-scale pressure tests are made on parts and portions of the building facade to see how the materials actually perform. This work is usually done during the construction phase by a curtain-wall testing establishment. The results of these tests will confirm the true performance of the cladding with respect to wind loads, air infiltration, water resistance, and combined stresses from wind loadings and structural movements.

3.4 VELOCITY PRESSURE

The pressure applied by the wind to a surface is called velocity pressure. This velocity pressure q_z at a height z may be calculated for design purposes from the formula

$$q_z = 0.00256K_z(IV)^2 \qquad (3.1)$$

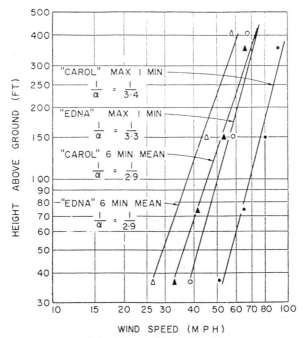

Fig. 3.3 Observations of hurricanes Carol and Edna (1954) at Brookhaven, Long Island. (Terrain is flat country with scrub trees.)

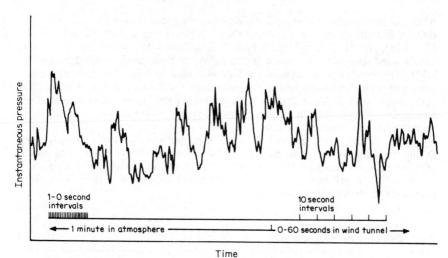

Time

Fig. 3.4 Diagrammatic trace of variation of surface pressure with time.

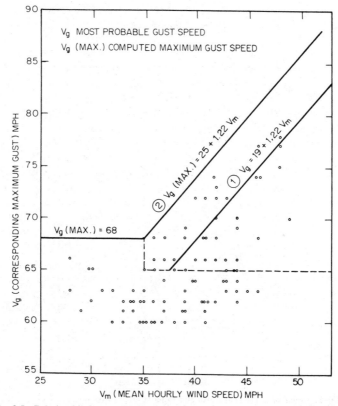

Fig. 3.5 Relationship between gust speeds of over 60 mph and mean hourly speeds.

where the basic wind speed V is selected from the basic wind speed map of the United States (Fig. 3.7) or from climatic data. The importance factor I is a constant referring to the relative importance of building use, and the velocity pressure exposure coefficient K_z is a constant referring to the severity of velocity pressure exposure. These are described in some detail in ANSI code A58.1 (1982).

One of the most important factors to be considered is the increase of the mean wind velocity with height. A corollary to this is the retarding effect of the surface friction on wind velocity nearer the surface. Various empirical, semiempirical, and theoretical formulas have been derived to represent the variation of wind velocity with height. For structural purposes the exponential or power-law profile has been used most widely because of its simplicity. It can be stated as follows:

$$V_z = kz^{1/a} \tag{3.2}$$

where V_z is the velocity at height z above ground and k and $1/a$ are constants.

By suitable choice of exponent this expression can be made to correspond closely over a considerable range to the other forms of profile which are less empirical. The power law is applicable only in the layer extending from the ground up to the height at which the gradient velocity is first attained [usually in the range of 305 to 610 m (1000 to 2000 ft)]. Above this height the wind velocity may

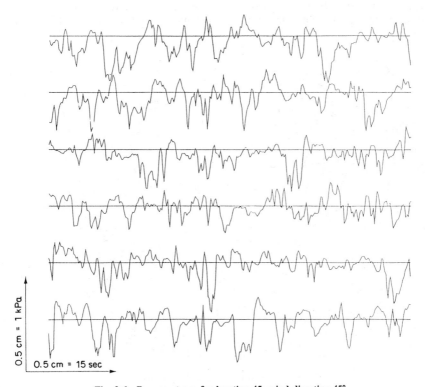

0.5 cm = 1 kPa

0.5 cm = 15 sec

Fig. 3.6 Pressure trace for location 45; wind direction 45°.

be regarded as constant. Notice that these profiles are affected by different types of surface roughness (Figs. 3.8 and 3.9).

In recent years the limits of wind tunnel testing and prediction of wind loadings on tall buildings have been vastly improved. This has been due to advances in the theory of fluid dynamics and the existence of wind tunnel testing laboratories using the low-speed, boundary-layer wind tunnels which are extensions of wind tunnels originally developed for aircraft design (Fig. 3.10).

The development of computer technology and miniature sensors, called transducers, has also made it possible to record, handle, and reduce all this information. Correlation between wind tunnel test results, using small-scale models of the building and its environment, have been confirmed by comparison with the actual pressures experienced on high-rise buildings. Further testing on full-scale portions of a particular building is used to confirm the actual performance of cladding and structural elements.

3.5 EFFECT OF GUSTS

As a result of the turbulence, which is both inherent in the airflow upstream and induced by the building itself, the readings will fluctuate with time, as was shown diagrammatically in Fig. 3.4. These fluctuations are best dealt with statistically, and each reading can be represented by a mean value, together with a fluctuating or gust component about that mean. The mean value is the average value over a sufficiently long period of time. Traditionally wind records are expressed in terms

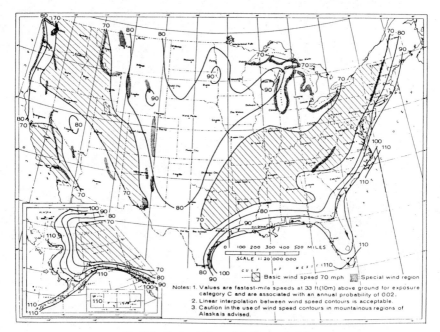

Fig. 3.7 Basic wind speed (miles per hour).

of 3-sec-gust speeds (which is the response time of the anemometer at a typical recording station), or mean hourly wind speeds, which are the average of the 3-sec values over a period of 1 hour.

It is apparent from Fig. 3.4 that the shorter the interval taken, the higher the maximum gust value will be. It is therefore necessary to determine an "average" interval that is appropriate to the way results are to be used. Thus, when considering wind loading on the building as a whole, only those eddies that are sufficiently large to act on all the building at the same time need be considered, and these are associated with a longer average interval. For the design of cladding, a shorter period must be used.

If the fluctuating component is considered as distributed about the mean value in accordance with the normal or gaussian distribution (Fig. 3.11), each reading can be described completely by its mean and standard deviation. In the wind tunnel test the readings are recorded by a minicomputer, which effectively calculates and stores these values as illustrated diagrammatically in Fig. 3.12. Figure 3.13 shows the Fisher-Tippet type 1 distribution.

3.6 BUILDING CODES FOR WIND LOADS

The local building codes used for design usually reflect the experience of what has already been built (usually smaller buildings) and how they reacted to local conditions over a longer period of time. Nationally recognized codes, such as the BOCA code (1990) and the ANSI code A58.1 (1982), reflect a broader range of conditions and engineering experience. Since the nature of the wind is modeled

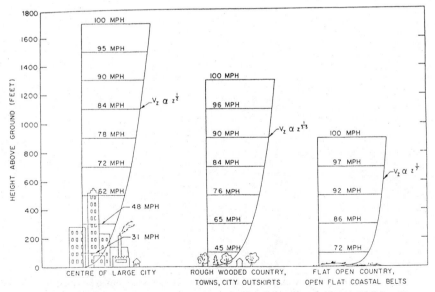

Fig. 3.8 **Velocity profiles over terrain with three different roughness characteristics for uniform-gradient wind velocity of 100 mph.**

by the terrain and by adjacent buildings, one can get a much better prediction of actual wind loading from a good wind tunnel test, particularly for larger high-rise projects or for buildings with unusual shapes.

Analytical procedures, such as the one recommended by ANSI code A58.1 (1982), may be applied to the majority of buildings and other structures, but the designer is cautioned that judgment is required for those buildings and structures having unusual geometric shapes, response characteristics, or site locations, for which channeling effects or buffeting in the wake of upwind obstructions may warrant special considerations.

External pressures, however, are not the end of the problem. One also has to take into account the internal pressures that can develop within the building, and this involves postulating an appropriate design scenario. If the cladding is designed to be effectively impermeable, is it necessary to consider the possibility of a significant opening occurring?

Another, and probably more fundamental, problem is the consideration of missile impact, which can be more critical than the design wind pressures that we are now able to determine in such a sophisticated way. This was well demon-

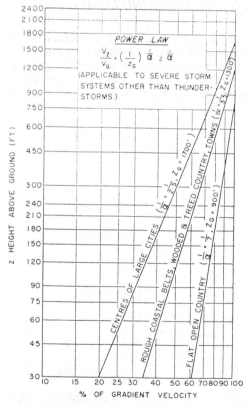

Fig. 3.9 **Increase of velocity with height over level ground for three different types of surface roughness according to power law.**

strated by hurricane Alicia, which devastated Houston in August 1983. Some codes, such as those in Australia, now include requirements in this regard.

The internal pressure of the building, for reasons mentioned, has to be considered in conjunction with external pressures from the wind. The difference, or potential difference, between external and internal pressures should be the design pressure to which the building cladding must respond. To this must be added an appropriate safety factor to allow for overstress and for statistical variations inherent in any prediction of this kind.

Different portions of the building envelope will respond differently to wind loadings. Since wind is applied in a series of gust pressures, with numerous peaks and valleys over time, different parts of the facade will react at different rates. For example, the steel or concrete structure of the building frame will require a longer period to react to a wind load than, say, a light metal panel or a sheet of glass. Therefore, the short-term loads or gust loads that must be successfully resisted by the cladding are much larger than those required for the basic structure of the building frame.

For cladding, these relatively high wind loads from gusts, together with any movements inherent in the building frame, must be anticipated. Also, the impact area of a short gust on the facade can be as small as a few facade elements, such as several mullions, lites of glass, panels, or frames. These have a very short natural dynamic response time compared to the building structure as a whole. Facade elements must respond to these higher gust loads.

3.7 VIBRATION OF STRUCTURES

Intimately connected with the subject of dynamically applied gust loads is the vibration of structures (Council on Tall Buildings, Group SB, 1979; Group CL,

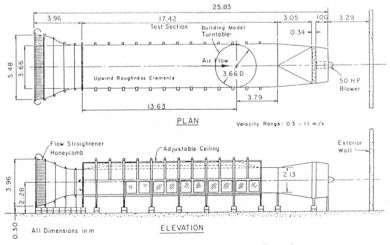

Fig. 3.10 Environmental wind tunnel configuration.

1980). Serious vibration, generally implying vibration at one of the natural frequencies of the structure, can arise in two ways:

1. Self-excitation, in which the form of the structural element is such that deflection to an applied wind force actually increases the wind force. This type of aerodynamic instability was true, for instance, of the section used in the deck of the Tacoma Narrows bridge, which failed dramatically.

2. Forced vibration due to instability in the flow pattern, induced by the shape of the structure itself or due to a natural periodicity in the airflow itself.

Often both these phenomena occur simultaneously.

As mentioned in Section 1.4, interaction between cladding and structure is a very interesting area. The cladding can affect the behavior of the structure in two primary ways—first, by adding stiffness, and second, by providing damping. Most authorities believe that the stiffening effect on nonstructural elements should be ignored in strength calculations under wind load, but could be of importance for seismic design.

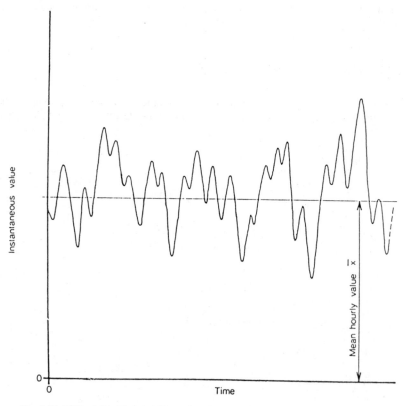

Fig. 3.11 Illustration of probability density function of fluctuating surface pressure.

3.8   *MEASUREMENTS AND DATA REDUCTION*

Having set up the wind tunnel, the various effects can then be measured in a
number of ways as follows.

1. *Anemometer readings.* Wind speeds on any point around the model can be
   measured using a hot-wire anemometer mounted on a probe. The probe is
   small enough not to disrupt the airflow significantly. These readings, however,
   are not of direct value for determining wind loading on buildings and are of
   more use in assessing environmental or local effects.

2. *Pressure readings.* The model can be fitted with pressure tapping points connected to a measuring device (Scanivalve) fixed below the base of the model, and
   these will measure the air pressures immediately adjacent to the tapping points.

3. *Balance readings.* The resultant forces and bending moments acting on the
   structure can be measured by mounting the model, or part of it, on a balance
   fixed below the base. In this test, only pressure readings are taken.

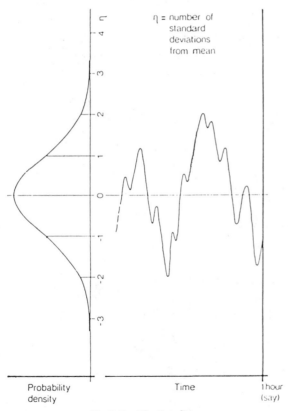

Probability   Time   1 hour
density   (say)

Fig. 3.11   (*Continued*)

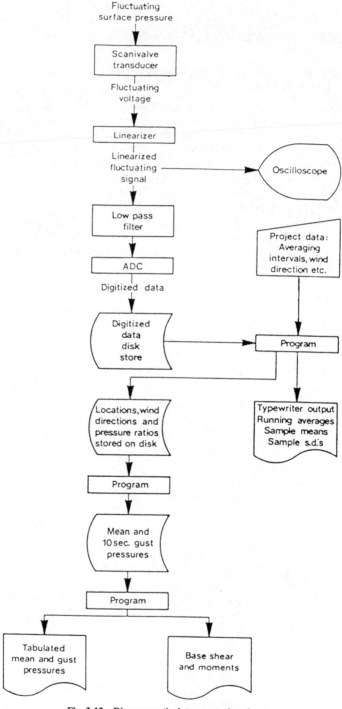

Fig. 3.12 Diagrammatic data-processing chart.

The interaction of the wind and the building form can be made visible in the wind tunnel by the use of a small movable jet of smoke, introduced into the wind stream next to the building. Motion pictures of this smoke stream are helpful in seeing the actual effects of the wind on critical portions of the structure, and in areas near pedestrian ways and outside people space.

Data are recorded, analyzed, and processed by an on-line computerized data-acquisition system. Pressure coefficients of several types are calculated by the computer for each reading on each tap and are printed in tabular form as computer readout. Using wind data applicable to the building site, representative wind velocities are selected for combination with measured pressures on the building model. The time selected for data integration may be checked to assure sampling from a uniform and consistent portion of the database (Fig 3.14). Instantaneous pressure coefficients are plotted against integration time.

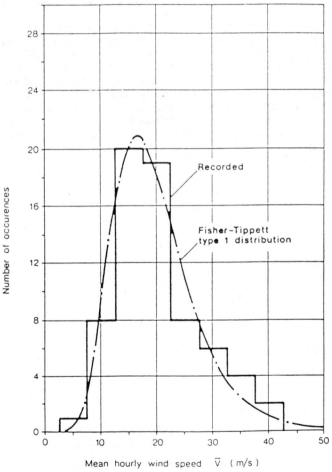

Fig. 3.13　Fisher-Tippett type 1 distribution.

The integration of test data with wind results in the prediction of peak local wind pressures for the design of glass or cladding may include overall forces and moments on the structure (by floor if desired) for the design of the structural frame. Pressure contours are then drawn on the developed building surfaces, showing the intensity and distribution of peak wind loads on the building (Figs. 3.15 and 3.16). Notice the presence of two local high-pressure spots, or hot spots, shown in Fig. 3.16. These results may be used to divide the building into zones where lighter or heavier cladding or glass may be desirable.

There is a zone of particular interest right next to the ground level, which affects pedestrians and the entrance areas. This zone can also be analyzed and detailed with smoke tests and by setting pressure taps in the pedestrian areas. Not only can the wind thus be predicted at the pedestrian areas, but also design elements such as baffles, canopies, and wind screens can be analyzed as they relate to the pedestrian environment. Terraces, plazas, some park areas, and other public spaces next to tall buildings frequently have unacceptably high winds, which can be studied here.

Based on the visualization (smoke tests) and on a knowledge of heavy pedestrian use areas, a dozen or more locations may be chosen at the base of the building, where wind velocities can be measured to determine the relative comfort or discomfort of pedestrians in plaza areas, near building entrances, near building corners, or on sidewalks. Usually a reference pedestrian position building area is better or worse than the environment a block or so away in an undisturbed area. In Figs. 3.17 and 3.18 mean velocities and turbulence intensities are charted at sample pedestrian locations. This information helps in controlling pedestrian areas and designing entrances and cladding at the ground floor.

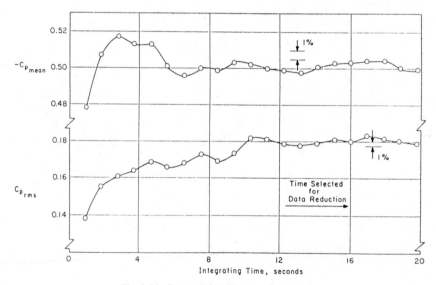

Fig. 3.14   Data sampling time verification.

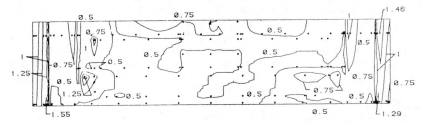

Fig. 3.15 **Peak pressure contours of base, north elevation; peak negative pressure coefficients.**

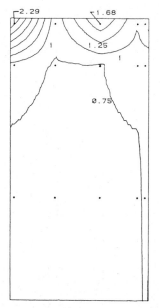

Fig. 3.16 **Peak pressure contours, showing "hot spots," of east tower, southeast elevation; peak negative pressure coefficients.**

3.9   WIND LOADINGS IN DESIGN

Design wind loads established from test data or from the building code are applied to different parts or portions of the project. For cladding it is also important to take into account any movements of the structural frame due to wind and other causes. The greatest wind pressures are usually negative and occur near corners on walls on the lee side of the building (Fig 3.19). The combination of maximum negative pressure plus the effect of internal pressures allowed by infiltration or by window failures will establish a maximum design load for the facade or cladding. The loss of internal pressure can increase stresses on the remaining cladding in the event of a failure of a leeward window unit in the facade.

Wind pressures are greatest near corners, sharp edges, and protrusions. These high-pressure zones can be as large as one-eighth or one-tenth of the width of the facade. The same situation occurs at the top edge of a building. Special effects are seen also along rounded or cylindrical shapes. Near sharp corners, a phenomenon called oscillating or shedding vortices may occur, and this can give very high pulsating pressures and reversals of stress. Areas located at or near the separation of flow or near the reattachment of wind flow are also subject to very high pressures and often form hot spots.

Different portions of a building frame and cladding will respond differently to wind loadings. The primary building structure or frame responds much more slowly to any gust due to its large mass and relatively slow dynamic response. It can take a minute or more for a large building frame to respond to a gust load, and in that time shorter gust have come and gone. Cladding or curtain-wall ele-

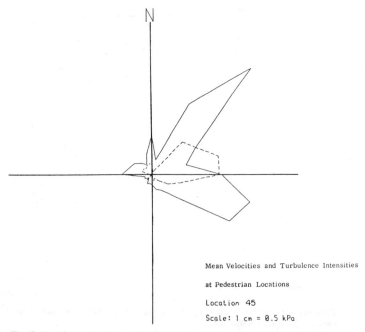

Mean Velocities and Turbulence Intensities

at Pedestrian Locations

Location 45

Scale: 1 cm = 0.5 kPa

Fig. 3.17 Mean velocities and turbulence intensities at pedestrian locations.

ments, on the other hand, have to withstand much higher gust pressures (of shorter duration) than the main structural frame. This is due to their smaller dimensions and faster dynamic responses compared to the main structural frame. Metal panels, aluminum framing members, and glass are affected more quickly by short gusts over smaller dimensions on limited portions of the facade (Figs. 3.15 and 3.16). Cladding elements do undergo continuous wind loadings and oscillations from both positive and negative wind forces (Fig 3.4). For that reason they and their anchors are subject to problems of fatigue and combined stresses in ways that the primary building structure is not.

In recent years, buildings have sometimes been too flexible for comfort and sway noticeably in high winds. This phenomenon is particularly evident on the upper floors of some office towers, to the point where such measures as tuned mass dampers have been installed to counteract the sway from the wind. For glass and other curtain-wall members there is a limit beyond which the perception of this motion to the building occupants is uncomfortable and disturbing. Panels that vibrate in the wind, mullions and glass that deflect in and out with amplitudes on an inch or more, and buildings that creak and groan in the wind are distinctly uncomfortable and sometimes frightening to their occupants.

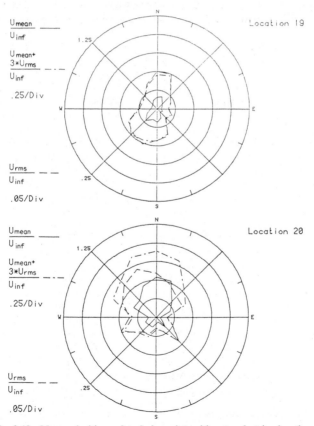

Fig. 3.18 Mean velocities and turbulence intensities at pedestrian locations.

There are buildings where elevator service is reduced or disrupted during high winds, and others where substantial cracks are evident in masonry and plaster walls and partitions due to wind deflections. On some of the lighter-weight reflective glass facades it is possible to see ripples of wind traveling across the entire facade of the building. Beyond the need for structural strength, a building has to provide a reasonable feeling of comfort and protection to its occupants. This can be directly related to adequate stiffness of structure and cladding beyond the minimum allowable for strength.

It is now possible to establish the acceleration due to wind gusts of a building structure. This is done in a wind tunnel. Limiting the allowable acceleration to a specified value limits the perceived motion of the building. The same design responsibility applies to pedestrian areas and entrances about the base of high buildings where wind effects can be controlled through design for comfort and protection.

3.10 FAILURES DUE TO WIND

Although structural failures are rare, wind-related cladding or curtain-wall failures are much more common. These failures are most often evident as glass breakage or anchor damage. Anchors are particularly susceptible to combined

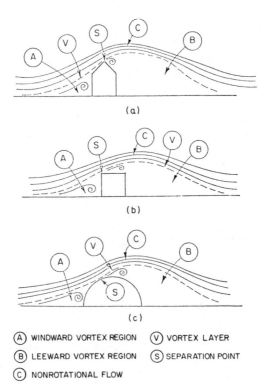

(a)

(b)

(c)

Ⓐ WINDWARD VORTEX REGION   Ⓥ VORTEX LAYER

Ⓑ LEEWARD VORTEX REGION   Ⓢ SEPARATION POINT

Ⓒ NONROTATIONAL FLOW

Fig. 3.19 Flow around three typical building shapes.

stresses and to unanticipated movements between curtain wall and building structure. With today's trends toward more flexible building frames and lighter curtain-wall elements, extra care is needed to predict and compensate for all movements affecting the cladding and the underlying building frame (especially since they do not always move together).

The design of stone and masonry elements, which are now becoming increasingly popular, requires special consideration and detailing to avoid failure from fracture. Masonry and stone are not perfectly elastic, and these materials will benefit from a design which reduces wind stresses by isolating them from structural movements and by taking advantage of pressure-equalized design principles.

Metal mullions and panels can fail in deflection, particularly in combination with gaskets, sealants, and glass. With the continuous pumping action of the wind, these assemblies can "walk" or flex out of position, inducing failures in gaskets, in sealants, and finally, in the glass. Even without major visible damage to its components, a building skin can be ruptured to the point of losing its watertight and airtight integrity. Brittle building materials such as masonry and stone are more subject to wind damage for the same reasons.

Progressive failure is one of the modes of failure that is of particular concern. This can happen with glass elements as it did during hurricane Alicia in 1983, or with the infamous case of the John Hancock building in Boston in the early 1970s. This also can happen to metal members, starting with mullion, panel, or anchor failure. Once it gets started, for whatever reason, progressive failure will continue over a considerable area by feeding on its own damage. Design measures can be taken to reduce these hazards.

3.11 THE ROLE OF SPECIALIST REVIEW

At present, the situation is often unsatisfactory in that the specification for cladding is developed by the architect, and specialists are quite often called in after bids have been received to evaluate proposals by the cladding manufacturer and, in some instances, to take on the responsibility for the building's structural and other performance. There is a strong opinion within the profession that a complete examination of this aspect should be performed early in the design phase, before design development is complete, and certainly before contract documents are made.

3.12 CONDENSED REFERENCES/BIBLIOGRAPHY

ANSI A58.1 1982, *American National Standard Minimum Design Loads for Buildings*
BOCA International 1990, *Basic Building Code*
Cermak 1971, *Laboratory Simulation of the Atmospheric Boundary Layer*
Cermak 1975, *Applications of Fluid Mechanics to Wind Engineering*
Cermak 1979, *Wind Engineering*
Council on Tall Buildings Group SB 1979, *Structural Design of Tall Steel Buildings*
Council on Tall Buildings Group CL 1980, *Tall Building Criteria and Loading*
Davenport 1960, *Wind Loads on Structures*

Davenport 1961, *The Application of Statistical Concepts to the Wind Loading*
Davenport 1967, *Gust Loading Factors*
Harris 1972, *Measurements of Wind Structure*
Lawson 1980, *Wind Effects on Buildings*
Penwarden 1975, *Wind Environment around Buildings*
Peterka 1983, *Selection of Local Peak Pressure Coefficients for Wind Tunnel*
PPG 1979, *PPG Thickness Recommendations to Meet Architects Specified One-Minute*
Reed 1983, *Wind Loading and Strength of Cladding Glass*
Shand 1985, *Glass Engineering Handbook*
Simiu 1975, *The Buffeting of Tall Structures by Strong Winds*
Simiu 1978, *Wind Effects on Structures*
Simiu 1984, *Ring-on-Ring Test and Load Capacity of Cladding Glass*

4

Design of Cladding
for Earthquakes

Of all significantly seismic countries with high rises, the United States and Japan probably have the most specific code provisions and research efforts regarding the design of cladding to withstand earthquakes. This discussion will therefore be based on the seismic design of cladding in these countries. Although the principles of cladding design for earthquake resistance are fairly consistent, the actual design criteria and detailing for mitigation of cladding failure vary widely from country to country, and even deviate to some extent among buildings in the same city. Beyond the specific engineering and building code issues, there are economic, architectural, production, and construction tradition realities which play a considerable role in the design process of cladding for earthquake resistance. This chapter integrates these technical and practical considerations in an overview of the subject. A detailed examination of earthquake loading and response can be found in Chapter 2 of Volume CL of the Monograph on Planning and Design of Tall Buildings (Council on Tall Buildings, Group CL, 1980).

4.1 INTERSTORY DRIFT

In the most common usage of the term, *cladding* implies that the wall components of the building envelope are not structurally designed to contribute to the overall lateral or gravity load capacity of a building. Although cladding is "nonstructural" in this sense, it in fact requires structural design and detailing in anticipation of gravity and lateral forces related to its own mass or geometry, such as thermal, shrinkage, wind, erection, and, in some cases, earthquake loads. In zones of high seismicity, this last design consideration is possibly the most crucial for mitigating potential property damage and life safety hazards.

Since tall buildings are usually designed to absorb some energy released by earthquakes through deformation of the structural frame, a fundamental design requirement of cladding is to accommodate that deformation. Tall building deformation is conveniently quantified in terms of interstory drift, or story drift, which is the relative lateral displacement between two adjacent levels. A more meaningful term, *story drift ratio,* refers to the ratio of story drift divided by story height. In current practice, the design of cladding to minimize earthquake damage focuses on detailing of the cladding and its connections to the frame, such that the cladding is effectively isolated from the frame, and story drift does not result in great stresses in the cladding or its connections. Building cladding typically has a relationship to its structural frame analogous to a vertebrate's relationship of its skin to its bones; if the vertebrate's skin were rigidly attached to the bones, the stresses resulting from movement and relayed to the skin would be a serious problem.

Some mid-rise buildings with structural frames do not have structurally detached cladding for an exterior wall system. Masonry infill walls of a concrete frame, for example, do not isolate the wall from the frame's structural response. As a result, in North Africa, Southern Europe, Central America, and South America, where such construction is common, major damage to these exterior walls, which show the classic X shear cracking, is ubiquitous after an earthquake. Ironically, these infill walls are sometimes an inadvertent saving grace in countries where concrete structural frames are not ductile and moment-resisting. The exterior infill wall interacts with the structural frame in providing lateral resistance like a shear wall—an effect that is probably not intentional by the designer, and certainly is not included in the calculations.

Although exterior building skins that are intentionally isolated from the frame are not designed to contribute stiffness to the building, they always do so to some degree. The measure of cladding's contribution to the building's lateral stiffness and resistance to drift has yet to become a routine part of cladding analysis and design because it is difficult to predict reliably. It is hoped that experimental studies may soon enable designers to take advantage of this source of drift control. Further discussion on the interaction between the structural frame and its cladding is found in Section 4.13.

4.2 ISOLATING CLADDING FROM FRAME MOTIONS

The critical concept for designers to realize is that the cladding design strategy to deter earthquake damage relies on detailing the connections between cladding and frame so that the cladding is isolated from the frame and its motions rather than rigidly attached to it. Assuming a typical high-rise cladding system of panels attached to the girders and columns of a steel or concrete moment-resisting frame, there are two major approaches to detailing cladding so that in an earthquake the building skin may move independently from the structural frame.

The first method relies on an in-plane translational action of panels, sometimes referred to as *swaying* motion, as opposed to the second method of accommodating story drift, which relies on an in-plane rotation action of panels, generally called *rocking* motion. These motions for panels, typically connected to the frame at girders defining one or multiple stories, are illustrated in Fig. 4.1 and described in the following.

Whichever motion is implemented to help panels accommodate the building frame movement, the connections of the panel to the structural frame must carry the dead load of the panel, provide some degree of freedom for the panel to move in-plane, independently of the structural frame, and restrain the panel's out-of-plane motion. In the United States, there are two kinds of attachments per panel which achieve these goals using the sway mechanism. The so-called lateral-stay connections at one girder level (in this case the top) are detailed to behave like flexible links in the panel plane, which permit the accommodation of the frame's story drift in the panel plane, while restraining, or staying, the panel's out-of-plane motion. The bearing connections are at the other girder level and are designed to carry the dead load and in-plane shear of the panel. Both must allow for construction tolerances. In the United States, cladding panels are usually designed with the bearing connections at the bottom and the lateral stay connections at the top. The reason for this arrangement is partly due to the general construction tradition of supports at the bottom and partly to the belief by some engineers that a suspended arrangement results in additional tension in concrete panels that should be avoided. (It is the opinion of some that in actuality, such tension should not be difficult to compensate for.) Depending on the shape and size of the panel, there may be several lateral connections; however, the overall support system should be designed so that it is statically determinate.

Accommodation of drift by use of the translation, or sway, mechanism is widely used in the United States and, until the early 1970s, was prevalent in Japan. In the United States, tall narrow units, such as column covers, are more frequently designed than wall panels to rotate in the rocking motion. Tall buildings had been prohibited in Japan until confidence in earthquake engineering permitted the construction of Tokyo's first high rise, the Kasumigaseki building, in 1969. For the first several years thereafter, Japanese emulation of U.S. technology and design practice included the seismic design of cladding. By 1971, the IBM headquarters building in Tokyo, designed and erected by Japan's largest architectural and construction firm, Nikken Sekkei, was the first to have rocking connections. The concept of this prototype connection is now universally applied in Japanese tall buildings. The IBM building had panels which had a large height

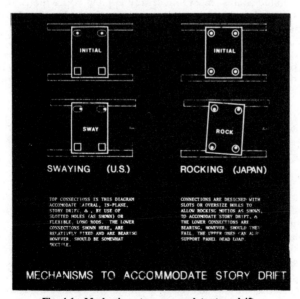

Fig. 4.1 Mechanisms to accommodate story drift.

compared to width. The engineers were concerned about the panel height resulting in exacerbation of differential frame-to-panel motion. While the common detail of a slotted angle with a short bolt "sliding" within the slot is limited in the
accommodation of bolt motion by slot length, the rocking mechanism uses details
that are not as constraining.

In the rocking mechanism, the joints all hinge to allow rotations of the panel
plane, resulting in a rocking motion to accommodate drift. Since the Tokyo IBM
headquarters building, rocking connections have developed into extremely sophisticated and complicated details, which are consistently more expensive than
translation connections. Both the additional expense and the ability of the connection to accommodate interstory drift stem from all four connections having
details that allow several controlled degrees of freedom between panel and frame.
Also, sliding connections that have acceptable reliability must be detailed carefully to avoid "sticking." The joints between the panels in either case, in theory,
do not suffer much distortion unless there is a difference in the connection lay-
outs of adjacent panels, as discussed in Sections 4.8 and 4.10.

4.3 CODE PROVISIONS FOR SEISMIC DRIFT

In both U.S. and Japanese building codes, seismic drift is specifically described
as a criterion for seismic design. In the *Japanese National Building Code,* current
requirements state that a drift limit of $1/200$ (or 0.005) times story height shall ordinarily be used for elastic design (Ministry of Construction, 1989). The code as-
signs an ultimate drift limit of $1/120$ times story height for buildings with a demonstrated tolerance for this greater drift. According to recent editions (since 1982) of
the western United States' most universally applied code, the *Uniform Building
Code* (UBC), the allowable drift is also set a $1/200$ times story height, unless it can
be shown that "greater drift can be tolerated" (ICBO, 1988).

Since localized cladding movement (panel-to-panel relative motion) is not the
same as the overall building motion in either degree or direction, drift requirements for cladding are distinct from drift requirements for the overall building.
The governing seismic drift requirement for cladding elements themselves is
stated in the 1982 and 1985 editions of the UBC with the provision that:

> Connections and panel joints shall allow for relative movement between stories of
> not less than...$(3.0/K)$ times the calculated elastic story displacement caused by re-
> quired seismic forces, or ½ inch whichever is greater,

where K is a horizontal force factor which reflects the lateral resisting system of
a building or other structure. The 1988 UBC has a similar requirement, calling for
the greater of 12.7 mm (½ in.) or $3(R_w/8)$ drift, where R_w is a numerical coefficient determined by the lateral load-resisting system.

Occasionally there is a need to consider a design both for a substantial wind
load and for seismic drift. Where both values are relatively close to each other in
magnitude, the seismic load is frequently binding only for basic structural and
public safety purposes, while the wind load must be resisted by all materials to
prevent damage not only to structural and cladding elements but also to the finishes. Where superficial damage may be tolerated from seismic disturbances,
wind loadings must usually respond to a stricter standard.

4.4 LATERAL FORCE COEFFICIENTS

In recent editions of the UBC, seismic force design values are determined from the formula

$$F_p = ZIC_p W_p \qquad (4.1)$$

Here, the seismic design force for the element under consideration, F_p is determined by the weight of the element, W_p, multiplied by a coefficient which is the product of the factors Z related to seismic zone, I determined from the importance of the building, and C_p depending on the type of nonstructural element under consideration. However, the tables of values given for these numerical coefficients, particularly in the case of the C_p factor, vary from edition to edition, resulting in different seismic design forces. It is important to note that larger seismic design force values are considered by some designers to not necessarily be more conservative. Lower values may well increase the probability of ductile connector yielding, rather than brittle, and thus exceedingly more dangerous, failure of welds, inserts, studs, or the panel material itself to accommodate drift.

4.5 RESEARCH FINDINGS IN THE SEISMIC PERFORMANCE OF CLADDING

General research into the performance of prototype connections and cladding panels has been rare. Tests are usually limited to the racking of isolated wall panel assemblages. The use of these tests, despite their unrealistic nature, is due to the cost limitations and analytical complexities of setting up full-scale tests which simulate the entire cladding and structure assembly. A notable exception to the usual isolated panel test was the use of full-scale laboratory studies of a test building in the U.S.-Japan Cooperative Research Program (carried out in Tsukuba, Japan) to assess the seismic performance of cladding and connections. This project is described in Section 4.6.

Computer and other conceptual modeling of nonstructural behavior is far more complicated and unreliable than that of just the structural frame. Thus analysis of potential cladding behavior by modeling is, for research purposes, most valuable as a supplement to physical testing. In design practice, such modeling of nonstructural assemblies such as cladding is rarely, though sometimes, carried out.

4.6 FINDINGS IN THE U.S.-JAPAN COOPERATIVE RESEARCH PROGRAM

In the 1980s, various projects on the full-scale testing of a six-story steel frame in the U.S.-Japan Cooperative Research Program examined crucial aspects of seismic design practice and codes in both countries. The full-scale steel frame provided an excellent opportunity to test cladding in a physical model that was much more realistic than the usual isolated racking tests. There were a variety of cladding panels constructed of precast concrete, glass-fiber-reinforced concrete, autoclaved lightweight concrete, and composite materials, which were designed according to U.S. or Japanese code and practice. The U.S. panels (which were mostly precast concrete or glass-fiber-reinforced concrete) were purposefully not all designed according to idealized practice, but were intentionally designed to just meet code requirements. All U.S. wall panels were designed with translating connections, while Japanese wall panels were designed with rocking connections.

For this part of the experiment, loading jacks at each level of the building applied one direction of horizontal displacements into the frame, which steadily increased up to a maximum story drift level of $\frac{1}{125}$. In both U.S. and Japanese codes, approximately this degree of drift is noted as requiring special justification. The applied static loading sequence culminated in a $\frac{1}{40}$ story drift ratio, which nearly reached the jacks' capacity and also closely corresponds to a credible drift in a major earthquake and to UBC design drift requirements. Imposed drift was about the same at each level throughout the sequence.

The U.S. connection details tested in the study are shown in Figs. 4.2 and 4.3. As already noted, typically, the translation mechanism is designed by the use of bearing connections, which carry the gravity load of the panel to the frame, and lateral connections, which have lateral degrees of freedom to accommodate interstory drift. These test panels reflected the common U.S. practice of bottom-bearing supports. However, the bearing and lateral connection locations vary from this common practice, depending on the configuration and proportion of the other panel shapes. For the basic rectangular wall panel attached to girders defining a story height, a potential problem occurs at these wall panels if and when the upper (lateral stay) connections fail completely, resulting in a panel's tendency to rotate outward and place an overwhelming moment on the bearing connections (Wang, 1986).

The rocking connections used in the test were typical of Japanese design practice. Considering their performance record in Tokyo high rises, numbering over 400 by now, rocking connections are excellent in accommodating drift, at least in moderate earthquakes. (A major event of the magnitude of the 1906 San Fran-

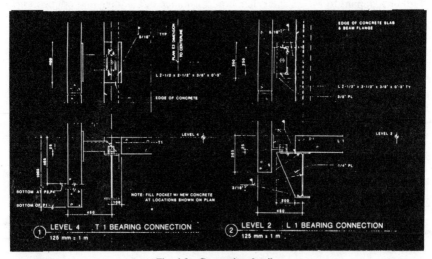

Fig. 4.2 Connection detail.

cisco or 1921 Tokyo earthquake has not yet imposed the ultimate test on build-ings designed in modern times.) This type of detail (Fig. 4.4) is rarely used in the United States and resistance to it will probably continue due to its complexity and expense. While U.S. engineers regard Japanese details to be overwhelming in these respects, on the other hand, Japanese engineers regard U.S. details as unsubstantial and primitive looking. Regardless of the lower cost and positive test results of some of the U.S. details, the appearance of these connections does not instill confidence in Japanese designers accustomed to the more substantial looking rocking details. Likewise, despite the excellent performance of Japanese cladding connections in the tests, this aspect of Japanese design practice is un-likely to be readily adopted by U.S. designers due to the daunting complexity of the Japanese details, which U.S. engineers associate with greater potential for malfunction.

4.7 SWAYING CONNECTIONS VERSUS ROCKING CONNECTIONS

From the result of the U.S.-Japan research, it appears that the translating or swaying mechanism is a viable way to accommodate story drift. However, the success of the mechanism is extremely dependent on the type of lateral and bear-ing connections used. Lateral connections which used long, ductile, steel rods (Fig. 4.5) to accommodate story drift have excellent performance in comparison to those using short steel rods fitted into slotted holes of steel angles. The prob-lems with the latter connection include insufficient slot length in the case of mas-sive story drift, and in other instances, factors which impede sliding, thereafter resulting in the early shearing off of the short connection rod. Such failure of the lateral sliding connection, in a life situation, is extremely dangerous, especially when the bearing connections are located at the bottom of the panel, and the en-tire unit is likely to flip outward from the building, possibly failing the bearing

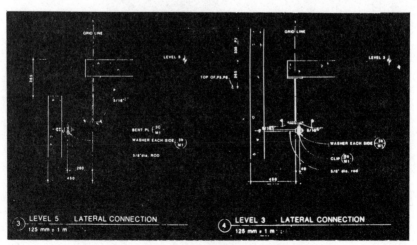

Fig. 4.3   Connection detail.

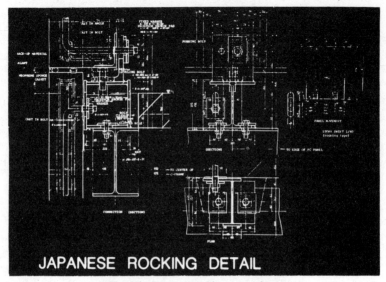

Fig. 4.4   Japanese rocking connection.

Fig. 4.5   Clip-angle and tube-type bearing connections.

connections as well. Figure 4.6, a photograph from the U.S.-Japan experiments, illustrates this potential failure. In practice, U.S. engineers are sometimes concerned about the effectiveness of sliding connections, especially after weathering with time might increase friction between the steel parts.

U.S.-type bearing connections also have a potentially dramatic effect on the performance of cladding in a major earthquake. Although these connections may show no signs of failure or even deformation in themselves, the flexibility and ductility of the connection affects the amount of stress conveyed to the surrounding panel. As a result, in the U.S.-Japan tests, a dramatic increase in concrete cracking occurred at panel locations where more rigid tube connections were installed, and little or no such cracking occurred where flexible clip angles were used as bearing connections. This contrast in the case of the two connections is shown graphically in Fig. 4.7. This diagram illustrates the relative degree of cracking in concrete at the elements with the tube versus the clip-angle bearing connections.

Japanese rocking connections have excellent behavior, assuming installation of the complex connection is correct. These connections depend on several working sliding connections—at least double the number required in the counterpart U.S. connection. Given extremely conscientious detailing of connections, Teflon washers, and low-friction metal, the sophisticated Japanese rocking connections have proved to work very well under laboratory conditions. The rocking

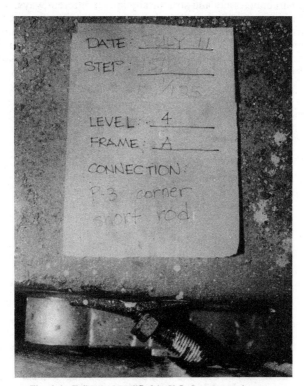

Fig. 4.6   Failure exemplified in U.S.-Japan experiments.

connection, in a real design situation, is susceptible to less than the perfect detailing that is mandatory for proper motion of the sliding mechanisms. Furthermore, under site conditions, the design to the connection would be more likely, than under controlled laboratory conditions, to allow a misinstallation of part of the assembly to go undetected. For example, even in the U.S.-Japan experiment, an early failure occurred in a Japanese rocking connection in which a slotted plate had been installed upside down. Similarly, if U.S. sliding connections are overtightened—a condition that is not apparent by merely looking at it—then the mechanism to accommodate story drift is rendered ineffective. These examples underscore the dangers of a detail's susceptibility to installation errors, especially when such errors are not easily spotted. Designers of these connections should strive to reduce such susceptibilities, especially when the experience and the reliability of the installation crew are not predictable.

4.8 EFFECTS OF ARCHITECTURALLY DETERMINED PANEL CONFIGURATIONS

Architectural design issues may have a dramatic impact on cladding performance as demonstrated by the comparison of corner cladding panel and attachment configurations. Building corners are particularly critical in their design for drift. They can be treated architecturally and structurally in two different ways, as illustrated in Fig. 4.8. In one case, panels will likely suffer no ill effects as a result of a mitered joint arrangement where each flat panel is attached to the frame in a consistent direction. The joints will, however, undergo enormous distortion. In the other case, an L-shaped (in-plan) column cover wraps around the corner of the building and is attached to the frame in two orthogonal directions. This logical

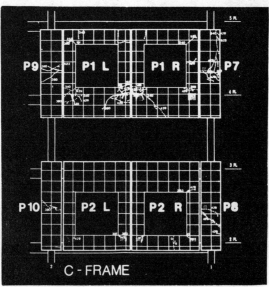

Fig. 4.7   Concrete cracking on panels.

expectation of panel performance was borne out by test results of the U.S.-Japan program. Figure 4.9 shows the cracking patterns of one side of the highly cracked L-shaped corner panels (P7 and P8) in contrast to the relatively unscathed flat panels (P4 and P6) at their respective corners of the test structure. The poor behavior of the L-shaped corner panel, which is often preferred for architectural reasons, indicates a need for designers to detail an alternative solution for both esthetic and seismic demands.

4.9 CONNECTION DUCTILITY

Ductility in detailing is another concept which is obvious in design philosophy but more elusive in practice since it is not calculated but rather assessed subjectively and comparatively. Comparing tube to clip-angle bearing connections, or long-rod to slotted angles with short-rod lateral connections, it is clear that designers should consider relative ductility as a prime structural goal.

4.10 PANEL AND JOINT KINEMATICS

Major joint distortions are a potential result in situations of high story drift where column cover panels, which are attached to columns, are next to typical wall panels, which are connected to girders. Even when the bearing and lateral connections on the column covers and wall panels are similar, there is a potential for straining joint material to the point where it necks in tension or squeezes out of the joint in compression, allowing impact between two panels. This effect is to be expected given the kinematics of adjacent panels with different geometries and

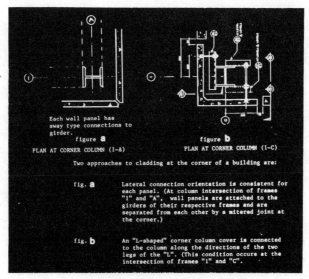

Fig. 4.8   Corner design and detailing.

different connection locations. The tendency toward this phenomenon was confirmed by instrumentation data, concrete panel cracking patterns, and photos of joint motion in the U.S.-Japan tests. It was found that the concrete panel and connections are extremely stressed as a result of panel-to-panel impact where adjacencies of panels with dissimilar motions exist.

4.11 GLASS CLADDING

Tall buildings have skins that consist of not only precast concrete, glass-fiber-reinforced concrete, or metal panels, but also of uninterrupted window walls of glass. This is the type of cladding which many laypersons as well as engineers are the most uneasy about. It is conceivable that while a structural frame is undamaged in an earthquake, giant shards of glass may hurtle from tens of stories onto people and streets below. These falling glass shards may also hit and fall against the remaining glass panels on the way down and create further breakage. If the glass that remains is even scratched, it can fail on the first wind or seismic loading thereafter, creating a scenario for progressive failure.

General (in other words, not building-specific) testing or research into glass window wall performance under seismic drift has been meager. The focus of glass cladding research has been on failures caused by wind pressure loadings normal to the surface and by shattering due to airborne fragments. Failure due to in-plane loadings on glass panels created by interstory racking in extreme wind or seismic events has received relatively minor attention. In the United States there have been investigations into deflections and rotations for panels tested under diagonal compression or buckling conditions, but no studies of the stress state and fracture pattern.

Racking tests on glass specimens for panels of various thicknesses, with adhesive film, were carried out at the Building Research Institute in Tsukuba, Ja-

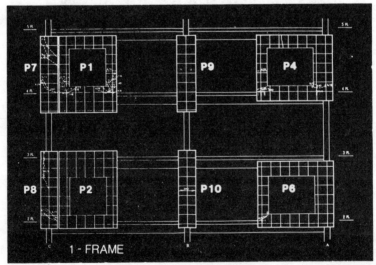

Fig. 4.9 Panel cracking patterns.

pan. (These films already exist for the purpose of controlling solar gain through window glass.) The recommended minimum thickness for the film was given as 50 μm. Aluminum sash local boundary conditions for float glass windows with tape, film, and wire were investigated. In all cases, cracks occurred. For the boundary conditions in which hard putty was used, glass fragments fell; for the elastic seal, glass fragments did not fall. It was recommended that balconies, ledges, or similar architectural features be used as a safety measure for pedestrians to stop the glass as it falls to the ground.

Recent laboratory results obtained in Yokohama, Japan, for diagonal compression and buckling of glass show that the fracture patterns under these conditions display numerous variabilities. Test were conducted on full-scale rectangular panels of equal dimensions except for the thicknesses of 2, 3, and 5 mm (0.08, 0.12, and 0.2 in.). The panels were loaded in-plane, the direction in which seismic loads are imposed on glass. Fractures appeared to start generally from the corners, with buckling occurring along the diagonal. The fracture patterns obtained resemble those found at the Tsukuba tests. Although similar in form, the fracture patterns for panels of different thicknesses displayed numerous variabilities. These fracture patterns differ from those obtained when panels are loaded by uniform pressure; the pattern can be used to identify the loading which induces failure. Other than this study, reports of the stress state induced in the panel under in-plane loading do not appear in the literature at this writing, although tests of panels under dynamic in-plane loadings are planned at the Institute for Disaster Research at Texas Tech University.

Research results have consistently shown that buckling failure is an extremely violent process, with glass fragments projecting rapidly from the window frame and traveling relatively large distances. Clearly this type of failure would represent a danger to building occupants at the window level as well as to pedestrians below and thus should be avoided if possible. The effects of both the glass panel and the framing design criteria on this failure mode should be studied. While it is recognized that tempered glass is stronger, it is also well known that the stronger glass will have a greater stored elastic strain energy and potential for devastation at failure. For this reason, untempered glass may have an advantage in this specific, seismic respect.

Pierced panels, which are panels that are cast or manufactured with a complete window opening, are not considered to be as problematic. Since rigid materials, such as concrete or metal, continuously surround the opening, the glass is protected from the immediate effects of interstory drift. The small amount of panel deformation transmitted to the glass is absorbed by detailing a space with elastomeric or other forgiving material around the window.

Geometrically, a number of other glass-to-nonglass cladding arrangements commonly exist. Spandrel glass between spandrel panels of concrete or metal is prevalent, especially from about a decade ago. In U.S.-Japan tests for a full-scale concrete building (prior to the tests for cladding on a steel frame), it was found that spandrel windows that were operable escaped damage, while otherwise identical but fixed sash windows broke. It appears that the operable sash not only permitted the window to be opened at will, but also provided the window with a means to accommodate the story drift of the building without failing. Unfortunately, modern tall buildings tend to have nonoperable windows in the interest of building economy and energy efficiency.

Similar tests for other framing systems, such as a braced steel frame, would be useful to the design profession. Guidelines for rehabilitation to panels in existing structures and for new construction should be based on studies on various framing types to determine critical locations for panels within the structure itself as well as an evaluation of the glass curtain-wall system.

Some cladding appears to be composed of pierced panel units, which are actually made up of T-shaped or L-shaped panels that are arranged to create fenestration by their juxtapositions. The purpose for this is economy in the production of these units and their erection. However, the impact of this arrangement on the vulnerability of glass to the story drift has not been studied. Since the fenestration openings are not completely enclosed by any one panel, it is likely that the glass would on occasion be subjected to and stressed by divergent behavior of the surrounding panels.

Based on a review of the aforementioned studies, recommendations for design procedures include the following: (1) replacement of local framing conditions in older buildings located in high-risk seismic regions; (2) changing design procedures for new structures to encourage the use of sliding local conditions; (3) use of laminated glass or adhesive window film for panels in sensitive locations; (4) use of balconies or other architectural features to stop the fall of glass debris if panels do fail during earthquakes; (5) as a precautionary measure, use of thicker panels for frames which are flexible; (6) use of untempered glass for high-risk seismic regions.

4.12 STONE VENEERS AND OTHER ATTACHED FINISHES

In the past decade, veneers such as stone regained much popularity in tall buildings in areas that include seismic regions in the United States and Japan. The trend was partly due to shifts in architectural taste, and which usually required a modern building to appear as though it were constructed of thick masonry. In reality, the stone veneer of such exterior walls is extremely thin relative to the thickness of the precast backing panel; the veneer is about 38 mm (1.5 in.) thick, depending on the type of stone, while the precast concrete behind it is about 127 mm (5 in.) thick. The thinness of the stone means a savings in cost, but also an increased risk of damage to the veneer. In the United States, veneer on later buildings tends to get thinner than that on the earlier buildings (which seemed to avoid damage under normal conditions), to the point where there are problems with bowing and other stone deformations even in the absence of earthquakes. Even if the veneer were sufficiently thick to resist normal stresses, the presence of an earthquake may severely tax the anchorages between the veneer and its precast concrete base. Typically, veneer is not directly bonded to the surface of the concrete. This is important because it reduces the problem of relative shrinkage and other stresses that would otherwise be transferred from the concrete to the facing, even in the absence of an earthquake.

In Japan, besides stone facing, ceramic tile facings on concrete panels are popular. The method of attachment is to place the tile in the precast mold with the backing toward the poured concrete. It is believed, and experience indicates, that this type of facing is potentially not problematic, even in a major earthquake.

4.13 INFLUENCE OF CLADDING ON DYNAMIC PROPERTIES OF FRAMES

By dint of its weight and distribution, cladding has proved to be the category of nonstructural elements having the most dramatic effect on a structure's dynamic properties such as damping and natural period. The impact of changes between the bare and the clad state of a structure on seismic performance is not ordinarily taken into consideration by designers, although the difference between translational frequencies of clad and bare structures could be in the range of 30% or more. Ignoring the possible building response effects of cladding on a structure, particularly with heavy panels, could be either conservative or liberal. On one hand, the added source of stiffness aids in drift control for both wind and earthquake loadings; on the other hand, dynamic response is complex, and besides the weight contribution of the cladding, it could adversely affect the total building response in indirect ways.

Lightweight cladding, such as metal panels or glass-fiber-reinforced concrete panels, may have advantages in seismic design, since these panels have low mass. The reduced weight of nonstructural elements may have beneficial effects for the design of the structure on the whole, as well as for the connections from panels to structural frame.

Studies on existing buildings and full-scale laboratory test structures in the United States and Japan have examined the effects of cladding on the structural properties of moment-resisting frames. In the late 1970s, experiments at the Georgia Institute of Technology showed the influence of cladding on a structure's frequencies, damping, and dynamic response in studies of two high-rise buildings in Atlanta, Georgia, while under construction (Goodno et al., 1983). Measurements of dynamic properties of building frames were taken as the cladding of the steel structure progressed. As part of the U.S.-Japan tests on a full-scale, six-story steel-frame building, ambient and forced vibration comparisons of behavior prior to and after the installation of cladding showed massive changes in stiffness properties between the naked frame and the clad frame with partitions and ceilings also installed.

4.14 DECISION-MAKING IN THE SEISMIC DESIGN OF CLADDING

The issues described thus far in the design of cladding for earthquakes are numerous in possible implications of structural behavior and nonstructural failure, and serious in terms of potential damage to property and casualties to people. The first decisions in design are, therefore, how the issues should be addressed, by whom, and in what sequence.

Design roles in building production can vary greatly from country to country. For example, in Japan the system of design roles for tall building projects is often very different from that in the United States. For high rises in particular, large Japanese design-construction firms not only carry a job through from early architectural conception to every detail of engineering, but also sponsor research into innovative design and detailing of aspects such as cladding to accommodate seismic drift. The reasons for the independent evolution of detailing and design roles in Japan and the United States include not only separation by the Pacific Ocean, but also separation by different languages, and by the focus on the immediate issues of the project at hand in structural design practice. Within a city, whether Japanese or American, variations in detailing reflect either the idiosyncrasies of the building or the philosophy of, and construction tradition familiar to, the designer.

The system of architectural and structural design handled by an architectural firm and a separate structural engineering consultant is commonplace in the United States in general, and in California, the most seismic of the contiguous states, in particular. Some U.S. firms combine architectural and engineering services (so-called A/E firms) and often specialize in tall buildings, such as the many offices of Skidmore, Owings, and Merrill. Under the usual U.S. system, neither architects nor structural engineering consultants design cladding and cladding connections inhouse. It is a task more commonly assigned to the precaster, the fabricator, or the cladding producer that has its own staff of engineers. This tendency reflects the U.S. design profession's perception of cladding as an independent and very specialized technical problem relative to the rest of the structural frame, particularly when potentially large lateral forces exist. Since the level of engineering capability of manufacturers can vary considerably, participation of architects and engineers is, in fact, quite important. A few U.S. offices, however, prefer to retain control of every aspect of the structural design of a building, including the full analysis and design, if not review, of cladding, connection, and anchorage designs that are produced by precaster, fabricator, or other cladding producer. Although this is a laudable approach, this practice appears to be decreasing.

4.15 CONCLUSION

For architects, the immediate issues of design tend to be esthetics and cost. It is not surprising that seismic considerations in the design of tall building cladding are far from prevalent among architects' concerns. While these emphases on appearance and budget cannot be faulted, it is important for architects and engineers alike to realize that the performance of cladding in earthquakes has an imminent impact not only on the potential damaged appearance and cost in repairs, but also on life safety. For engineers, the design of cladding and its connections may be simply an issue of satisfying the code and carrying out calculations correctly. Good design of these elements in seismic zones, however, ideally takes into consideration not only the basic code requirements but also the esthetic goals of the architecture; the minimizing of potential construction errors, particularly those that are invisible upon cursory inspection; the life safety issues that are not quantified in the building code; and the ductility of critical connections. A designer's awareness of seismic issues early in a project may well lead to cladding systems that do not compromise esthetics or economy, and also will make the proper seismic engineering of cladding easier to accomplish.

4.16 CONDENSED REFERENCES/BIBLIOGRAPHY

AIJ 1985, *Recommendations for Aseismic Design and Construction of Nonstructural*
Bouwkamp 1961, *Behavior of Window Panels under In-Plane Force*
Council on Tall Buildings Group CL 1980, *Tall Building Criteria and Loading*
Goodno 1983, *Cladding Structure Interaction in Highrise Buildings*
ICBO 1988, *Uniform Building Code*
Ministry of Construction 1989, *Japanese National Building Code*
PCI 1977, *Structural Design of Architectural Precast Concrete*

Phillips 1982, *Plant Cast, Precast and Prestressed Concrete: A Design Guide*
Reed 1985, *Glass Cladding Design for Tall Buildings*
Reed 1986, *Cladding Design for Tall Buildings*
Reed 1987, *An Expert System for Glass Cladding Risk Assessment*
Sack 1981, *Seismic Response of Precast Curtain Walls in Highrise Buildings*
Sakamoto 1984, *Proposals for Aseismic Design Method on Nonstructural Elements*
Shinkai 1984, *Interim Summary Report on Tests of a Seven Story Reinforced*
Wang 1986, *U.S. Side Final Report: Nonstructural Element Test Phase*
Wang 1987, *Cladding Performance on a Full Scale Test Frame*

5

Testing Cladding Systems

An in-depth discussion of all of the types of testing likely to be required on the plethora of cladding materials used on high-rise buildings would be an unrealistic task. This discussion simply identifies some of the more important tests that should normally be considered for cladding systems on high-rise buildings. It discusses the conflicting opinions where alternative test methods are available and, it is hoped, will convince some architects who are still reluctant to specify appropriate tests that a comprehensive testing plan is a prerequisite to successful cladding design and installations on high-rise buildings.

A comprehensive testing program for a high-rise cladding system should consist of at least the first two of the following three distinct phases:

1. Preconstruction testing
2. Quality control testing during construction
3. Limited postconstruction testing

5.1 PRECONSTRUCTION TESTING

Preconstruction testing is intended to verify that the specific materials and components being proposed by the selected contractor are in accordance with the project specifications. Once cladding is in place, repair can be both very expensive and very difficult, if not impossible. So preconstruction testing should be performed prior to the installation of critical cladding items on a building.

Since some materials must be cured for a considerable period of time before testing, it is normally desirable to begin preconstruction testing as soon after the award of the contract as possible. Despite the confidence of performance portrayed in most promotional literature, it is unwise to assume that all proposed materials are always going to perform according to the specifications.

Preconstruction testing almost always will include testing of the individual materials which comprise the cladding system. In many cases this includes the testing of sample areas of a cladding mock-up in advance of the general construction. For some items, the specifications require the contractor to obtain samples of the proposed materials and to send them to an independent laboratory, approved by the owner, for testing. For other items, the suppliers are allowed to submit written certification that the materials they are providing will conform to the specifications. Materials which normally require a supplier to provide written certification are not discussed in this chapter. What follows addresses only cladding materials which are required to be submitted to an independent laboratory for testing.

The testing laboratory selected should have extensive experience in testing the specific materials submitted. Frequently it is necessary to retain different laboratories for different portions of the testing. Following are guidelines for working with various types of materials. Reference to particular standards used in the United States, developed by the American Society of Testing and Materials (ASTM), is made in some examples.

1 Metal Panels and Members

Materials used in cladding systems consisting of metal panels and metal members, no matter whether steel, aluminum, or other metals, are seldom independently tested for specific projects. Certificates of conformance are normally sufficient. The exceptions would be any special coatings which are not the fabricator's standard finish or which have only a limited performance history. In these cases, accelerated weathering tests are sometimes specified, but the time constraints of most construction schedules allow only fairly limited aging tests to be performed. For this reason, deviating from standard coatings is not encouraged.

2 Brick and Block Masonry

Materials used in masonry cladding systems on high-rise buildings are usually tested rather than relying on certificates of conformance. Clay bricks are normally tested for compressive strength, 24-hour cold-water absorption, 5-hour boil absorption, saturation coefficient, and initial rate of absorption in accordance, in the United States, with ASTM C67 (1990). Concrete masonry units are normally tested for compressive strength and water absorption in accordance with ASTM C140 (1990).

Certificates of performance are normally accepted for mortar ingredients and grout ingredients, but after mixing, mortars and grouts are normally tested for compliance with the specifications. Mortars and grouts for clay brick masonry are normally tested for compressive strength, water retention, air content, and efflorescence. Mortars and grouts for concrete block masonry are normally tested for compressive strength and water retention in accordance with ASTM C780 (1990).

3 Stone Masonry

In high-rise buildings, stone cladding is normally cut as thin as acceptable performance will allow for weight reduction. Many stones which performed well in the past, when pieces were thicker, perform unsatisfactorily when cut thin. The kinds of stones most commonly used successfully as thin cladding are granite, limestone, marble, sandstone, and slate, but all types of stones should be tested specifically for each project. Building stones are a product of nature, and their physical properties can vary widely, even among stones removed from the same quarry.

As a minimum, tests should be performed to verify that the physical properties of the stone being considered satisfy the minimum requirements of the applicable codes and standards. Most standards specify minimum requirements for absorption, density, compressive strength, modulus of rupture, and abrasion resistance. For the designer, flexure strength tests on samples of the same thickness as proposed may be more meaningful than modulus-of-rupture tests. It is important to determine the strength of stones at attachments as well as their overall strength. Special tests of attachment details are frequently desirable.

Additional tests may also be warranted for some types of stones based on their performance record. For example, fine-grained, relatively pure marbles should be cycled through heating and wetting under controlled temperatures, simulating wall gradient conditions, to determine their susceptibility to bowing in service. Figure 5.1 shows an example of a stone which was cut too thin and has bowed in service. Granites with thermally finished surface treatments should be tested to ensure that they do not possess porosity-permeability relationships that render them vulnerable to damage by cyclic freezing. Depending on how thin they are going to be cut, it may be prudent to test some types of granite, sandstone, limestone, and marble for water permeability.

4 Concrete

Certificates of performance are normally accepted for the concrete ingredients. As a minimum, the concrete itself should be evaluated based on tests to measure

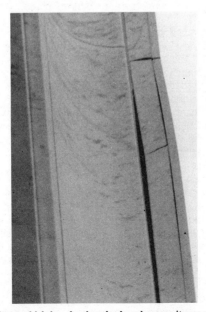

Fig. 5.1   Stone which has developed a bow because it was cut too thin.

slump, air content, unit weight, and compressive strength. To evaluate the durability of the concrete, it is necessary to remove cores from sample pieces to determine the air-void content and parameters of the air-void system, in accordance with ASTM C457 (1990) in the United States.

To evaluate the need for applying clear coatings, water absorption tests should be performed to determine the potential for weather staining of exposed surfaces, as described in the Prestressed Concrete Institute manual for quality control (1977).

5 Sealants

Submittals of certificates of conformance to appropriate ASTM standards are frequently all that are specified for sealants, primers, and cleaners. On high-rise buildings, however, where exposures are likely to be very severe, it is probably warranted to consider performing peel tests of sealant on samples of all materials to which the sealants will be required to bond. (See also Chapter 2.) Specified cleaning and priming procedures and products should be used. Lap joints that undergo a shear-type movement exert a peeling action on the bond surface which none of the standard tests simulate. The peel test, as described in ASTM C794 (1990), can provide an indication of sealant strength. On high rises it is also desirable to perform preliminary tests to evaluate the effect of priming surfaces to be caulked if the manufacturer considers it optional.

6 Cladding Mock-ups

Preconstruction testing of sample areas of cladding, mocked up in advance of general construction, can bring to light both design and construction weaknesses. The tests can also measure the performance of the cladding to determine whether or not the specified performance levels have been met.

When construction scheduling permits, it is normally more desirable to install a selected portion of the cladding system on the actual building as the mock-up to be tested rather than to build a mock-up in the laboratory. In the laboratory it is difficult to reproduce the cladding exactly as it will be installed on the building, duplicating the conditions of support, attachment, and continuity with other components.

Mock-ups on the building frequently have the advantage of revealing problems caused by unanticipated construction anomalies or tolerance variations of the building structure which the cladding system must accommodate. Mock-ups also are useful for evaluating visual acceptability and to serve as an approved record for the remainder of the job.

If quality control testing and postconstruction testing are specified for the project, there is an even greater advantage in specifying preconstruction testing on the actual building rather than in the laboratory because the same apparatus can be used for the later testing as well. When testing on the building, costs will be reduced and there will be less opportunity for claims of test procedure variations if production areas of cladding fail to pass quality control tests.

The mock-up, whether in the laboratory or on the building, should be of sufficient size to include all major elements, perimeter components, and expansion joint types. A mock-up two stories high by two bays wide which includes a corner is frequently specified.

Almost any performance criteria can be tested on cladding mock-ups. The following three criteria are of most common concern:

1. Structural adequacy of cladding system under wind load
2. Effectiveness of cladding system in controlling water penetration
3. Ability of cladding system to resist air leakage

Other criteria which are sometimes desirable to test for include condensation resistance, overall thermal transmission, sound transmission, and resistance to seismic loads.

7 Air Infiltration Testing

When testing a selected portion of the cladding on the building as a mock-up, the testing should be performed in accordance with ASTM E783 (1990). If it is necessary to perform the tests on a mock-up in the laboratory, the tests should be performed in accordance with ASTM E283 (1990). Air infiltration tests should normally be performed prior to water penetration tests because water trapped in the cladding tends to reduce air leakage.

8 Water Penetration Testing

When testing of a selected portion of the cladding on the building as a mock-up, the water infiltration testing should be performed in accordance with AAMA 501.3 (1987b). This method covers the determination of the resistance of installed cladding systems to water penetration when water is applied to the outside face simultaneously with a static air pressure at the inside face which is lower than the static air pressure at the outside face. Figure 5.2 shows an air and water infiltration test being performed at the site.

Fig. 5.2 Air and water infiltration test being performed in the field.

If it is necessary to perform the tests on a mock-up constructed in the laboratory, the water penetration tests should be performed in accordance with ASTM E331 (1990). This method, like AAMA 501.3, tests the resistance of the cladding system to rain penetration by creating a uniform static air pressure difference between the inside and the outside.

Another laboratory method is available which tests the resistance of a cladding system to wind-driven rain penetration by using an aircraft engine to produce a pressure on the outside wall surface. When using this method, interior finishes should not be installed as part of the mock-up because they will interfere with the ability to detect water leakage through the cladding during the test.

It is desirable to perform the preconstruction water penetration test twice, once before and once after the structural adequacy test is performed in order to get an indication if water penetration is likely to increase during service.

If water penetration problems are revealed in brickwork or concrete block work portions of a cladding system, the performance of the masonry can be evaluated separately by performing ASTM E514 (1990). Criteria for rating the performance of masonry walls are provided as part of the test. Figure 5.3 shows an E514 test being performed on a brick wall.

9 Structural Adequacy Testing for Wind

The strength and stiffness of framing for cladding members may be determined by engineering analyses, and deflections of glass and panels may be predicted by

Fig. 5.3   Field-modified version of ASTM E514 water permeability test being performed.

available data. However, performing a structural adequacy test is much more precise. The action of the composite assembly under loading can better be determined by tests because of the unpredictable performance of items such as sealants and gaskets, and because of the difficulty in anticipating the interaction of component parts.

A standard test procedure is available for the testing of cladding systems constructed of metal and glass. They may be tested in accordance with ASTM E330 (1990), which utilizes a load factor of 1.5. As discussed in Chapter 3, it is important that both negative and positive pressures be considered. Figure 5.4 shows a single window-spandrel section, Figure 5.5 a three-story section of curtain wall being tested. Cladding systems which contain combinations of materials requiring different factors of safety may require supplemental testing of some components to get a complete confirmation of structural adequacy.

As an example, a metal and glass cladding system with stone-spandrel panels should first be tested in accordance with ASTM E330 (1990) to confirm the adequacy of the metal components. Additional stone-spandrel panels should then be tested separately in accordance with ASTM E72 (1990) at a higher loading to confirm that the required higher safety factors for stone are available.

10 Condensation Testing

Condensation may be of particular concern in cold climates in high-rise buildings where high relative humidities occur naturally or are maintained intentionally. When condensation resistance tests are appropriate, they should be performed in

Fig. 5.4 One-story section of curtain wall being load-tested.

accordance with AAMA 1502.7 (1987b). These tests are normally performed on a laboratory mock-up and compare the cladding system to information on condensation on the inside surfaces when exposed to a set of standard test conditions.

11   Overall Thermal Transmission Testing

Most manufacturers and trade associations have thermal transmission figures for their specific materials. The actual thermal transmission performance of cladding systems is much more difficult to determine accurately, however, since usually the systems are fabricated using a combination of materials and they contain a variety of joints.

Thermal transmission tests normally have to be performed on laboratory mock-ups. Guarded or calibrated hot-box tests, performed in accordance with ASTM C236 (1988) or ASTM C976 (1990), respectively, may be used to measure the thermal transmission of any cladding system for which it is possible to build a reasonably representative mock-up of the size appropriate for the apparatus. Cladding samples up to 1.5 by 1.5 m (5 by 5 ft) can be accommodated in most guarded hot boxes, and samples up to 2.4 by 2.4 m (8 by 8 ft) in most calibrated hot boxes.

Hot boxes determine thermal performance by making measurements after establishing and maintaining a desired steady-state temperature difference across

Fig. 5.5   Three-story section of curtain wall being load-tested.

the mock-up for the period of time necessary to ensure constant heat transmission. Figure 5.6 shows a hot-box test being performed.

For cladding systems of glazing or opaque panels which have relatively high conductivity and where the air films contribute significantly to lowering the overall coefficient of thermal transmission, AAMA indicates that test 1503.1 (1987a) can be used as an alternative to hot-box testing.

Steady-state testing, although very useful for glass, metal, and thin-stone cladding systems, does not take into account the capacity of the heavier cladding systems to absorb, store, and release heat slowly, helping the building to remain cool during the day and warmer at night. It is not unusual for this time-lag effect to reduce energy consumption by 20%. Dynamic thermal tests are performed using a specially instrumented calibrated box capable of metering heat flow in both directions through the cladding. There are very few laboratories which are equipped to perform dynamic tests, and the costs for such tests are considerably higher than those for steady-state tests.

12 Seismic Testing

While there are numerous design guidelines, there are no standard methods for testing cladding systems for seismic performance. The forces and distortions that a building system experiences during an earthquake depend very strongly on its dynamic behavior, that is, not only on its natural period and damping but also on the manner and extent to which it yields. Experience has shown that it is generally not economically feasible to design buildings to remain elastic during the level of ground shaking that must be considered possible.

Should an extremely large earthquake occur, most high-rise structures are expected to yield, but must remain stable. The *Uniform Building Code* (ICBO, 1988) requires that deformation capability be considered for lateral deformations three to four and one-half times the values determined from the design forces, and special provisions for exterior elements require that the connections be designed to allow for these anticipated interstory drifts without causing brittle fail-

Fig. 5.6 Thermal test being performed in a hot box.

ure. The requirements of the seismic provisions can usually be substantiated by means of calculations and illustrative details on the construction drawings. When conformance to the seismic provisions cannot be thus substantiated, testing may be required.

Normally it is sufficient and more economical to mock up and test critical elements of the cladding system separately rather than to construct and test a whole cladding assembly. However, there may be cases where whole assemblies consisting of one or several precast elements must be tested. The test procedure should be developed or approved by the structural engineer of record to assure simulation of the conditions covered by the seismic design requirements. A properly developed mock-up should include in-plane racking distortions and out-of-plane distortions representing, at a minimum, interstory drifts three to four and one-half times the calculated displacements caused by the required (design) seismic forces. The tests should include cyclic displacements to simulate earthquake-caused motion. The results of the tests should be able to show that the connections will permit the required movement by sliding within slotted or oversized holes, or by the bending of steel with sufficient ductility capacity. In addition, if sufficient clearance between adjacent elements is not maintained, tests should demonstrate the ability to withstand the effects of interaction between the elements without creating a hazard.

5.2 QUALITY CONTROL TESTING DURING CONSTRUCTION

Quality control testing is intended to confirm that the quality of the materials and components approved by preconstruction testing continues to be provided during the course of construction. Quality control testing of individual materials should always be done on high-rise buildings, and frequently the testing of some representative areas of the in-place cladding system should also be done.

Generally, the same tests which were used to verify the adequacy of materials prior to construction should be used to verify that the materials provided during construction continue to satisfy the specifications.

1 Metal Panels and Members

The only quality control testing normally considered during construction is the testing of special coatings.

2 Brick and Block Masonry

During construction, it is common practice to use the compressive strength of the brick or block and the compressive strength of mortar as the quality control factors. Test results are to meet the specified ASTM requirements. Normally five brick or block and three mortar cubes are tested for each 100,000 brick or block laid.

Because flexure strength and water permeance are considerably more meaningful to the performance of masonry cladding systems than compressive strength, the designers of significant structures may give consideration to specifying the testing of sections of masonry rather than specifying compressive tests of units and mortar. Brick or block prisms can be constructed in accordance with ASTM E518 (1990) and tested to monitor masonry flexure strength. Figure 5.7 shows a flexure test in progress. Sections of masonry cladding can be tested for water permeance right on the face of the building in accordance with a field-modified version of ASTM E514 (1990).

3 Stone Masonry

Because of the variable nature of stone, it is often desirable to perform a set of tests on every fifth rough stone block cut from the quarry to verify its physical properties. If consistently acceptable results are obtained, it may be possible to reduce the frequency of testing, but it is seldom wise to stop testing completely. The quality control tests should include absorption, density, compressive strength, modulus of rupture, and abrasion resistance.

On the rare occasions when stone cladding on high rises is constructed with mortar joints instead of sealant joints, it may be desirable to perform flexure strength and water permeability tests similar to those recommended for brick and block masonry.

4 Concrete

It is normally desirable to perform quality control tests to verify the slump, air content, unit weight, and compressive strength during the casting of concrete cladding elements. One set of tests should be performed every day for each type

Fig. 5.7   Flexure test of masonry prism.

of concrete used. The tests should be performed in the same manner as the preconstruction tests.

5 Sealants

The only quality control testing normally desirable is to perform peel tests at regular intervals during the course of construction.

6 In-Place Performance Testing

In-place performance tests are relatively expensive. Therefore few can be justified on even the most prestigious project. However, not many tests are required to have a very positive effect on the quality of workmanship. One test performed soon after work begins and two or three additional tests performed during the remainder of construction are often sufficient. These are especially effective if the construction crew knows that the additional tests will be performed at unspecified times and unspecified locations.

   Water penetration and air infiltration tests are the tests most frequently used for quality control purposes during construction, first because these are the items most likely to fail to meet specifications and second because they are more economical to perform than most of the other tests on full assemblies.

   Field tests can be set up to confirm the performance of almost any cladding system characteristic in the event that conditions are observed that justify their performance. The specifications should clearly state that if any area of cladding fails to pass a quality control test, in addition to the cost of repairs, the contractor shall also be required to pay for the cost of the retesting.

5.3 LIMITED POSTCONSTRUCTION TESTING

At present, very little postconstruction testing is done except when a problem develops and its cause must be determined. It would be very desirable, however, to perform a few in-field performance tests on the building after the cladding system has been in service for about 10 months and before the normal 1-year warranty period runs out.

5.4 CONDENSED REFERENCES/BIBLIOGRAPHY

AAMA 1987a, *Aluminum Curtain Wall Design Manual*
AAMA 1987b, *Guide Specifications Manual*
ASTM C67 1990, *Standard Test Methods of Sampling and Testing Brick and Structural*
ASTM C140 1990, *Standard Methods of Sampling and Testing Concrete Masonry Units*
ASTM C236 1988, *Standard Test Method for Steady-State Thermal Performance of Build-*
ASTM C457 1990, *Standard Practice for Microscopical Determination of Air-Void Content*
ASTM C780 1990, *Standard Test Method for Preconstruction and Construction Evaluation*
ASTM 794 1990, *Standard Test Method for Adhesion-in-Peel of Elastomeric Joint Sealants*

ASTM C976 1990, *Test Method for Thermal Performances of Building Assemblies by*
ASTM E72 1990, *Standard Methods of Conducting Strength Tests of Panels for Building*
ASTM E283 1990, *Standard Test Method for Rate of Air Leakage through Exterior Win-*
ASTM E330 1990, *Standard Test Method for Structural Performance of Exterior Windows,*
ASTM E331 1990, *Standard Test Method for Water Penetration of Exterior Windows, Cur-*
ASTM E514 1990, *Standard Test Method for Water Penetration and Leakage through Ma-*
ASTM E518 1990, *Standard Test Methods for Flexural Bond Strength of Masonry*
ASTM E783 1990, *Standard Method for Field Measurement of Air Leakage through In-*
ICBO 1988, *Uniform Building Code*
PCI 1977, *Structural Design of Architectural Precast Concrete*

6

An International Perspective on Innovations in Cladding Materials and Systems

In addition to being aware of how to select materials, design systems, seal joints, and test cladding systems, it is important to look at past, current, and potential future innovations in cladding. This chapter provides an international look at both historic and state-of-the-art cladding technology. In 1980, Volume SC of the *Monograph on Planning and Design of Tall Buildings* reported that curtain walls of tall buildings were almost exclusively of metal construction (Council on Tall Buildings, Group SC, 1980). That is no longer the case. Of particular interest today are the many types of stone and glass that are also being used, as well as recent innovations in ceramic panel cladding materials. Several of these are discussed in the following sections.

6.1 JAPAN

Innovations in Japanese building skins date back to traditional Japanese wood buildings supported by a timber frame of columns and beams (Fig. 6.1). In this type of construction, the walls are hung on the frame and could technically be classified as early curtain walls.

Although Mies van der Rohe drawings and building images were available in Japan prior to World War II, industrialized and prefabricated curtain-wall technology was not introduced in that country until the 1950s. Figure 6.2 shows an early example of a metal and glass Japanese curtain wall. By the 1960s precast concrete curtain-wall technology borrowed from other countries was common practice, but it was not until the 1970s that many new techniques for improved curtain-wall design were actually developed in Japan. A "rocking mechanism," designed by Nikken Sekkei and described more completely in Chapter 4, was developed to accommodate the story drift affecting the large height-to-width ratio of the precast concrete panels used in the IBM headquarters building in

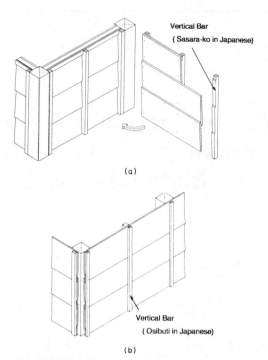

Vertical Bar
(Sasara-ko in Japanese)

(a)

Vertical Bar
(Osibuti in Japanese)

(b)

Fig. 6.1   Cladding of traditional Japanese timber frame buildings.

(a)

(b)

Fig. 6.2   Early examples of curtain walls in Japan.

104

Tokyo. Figure 6.3 shows the potential relative displacement of the cladding panels, while Fig. 6.4 illustrates the actual attachment mechanism.

Creativity in Japanese tall buildings cannot be studied without paying special attention to the skill and craftsmanship present in some very uniquely detailed works of architecture. Integrated systems design is always paramount to the success of a project. For the proper functioning of systems to occur, however, it is

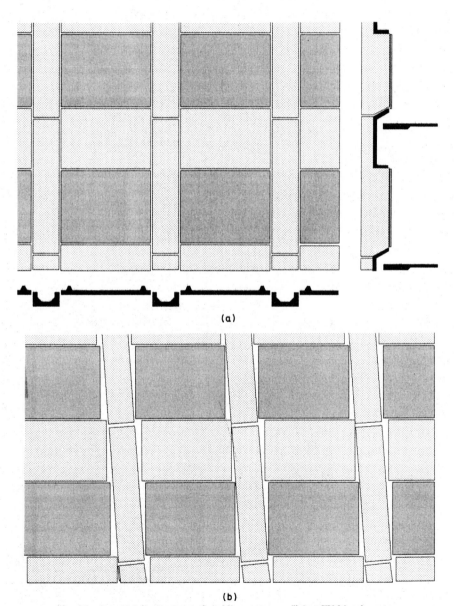

(a)

(b)

Fig. 6.3 Potential displacement of cladding system on Tokyo IBM headquarters.

necessary to understand the design and performance potential offered by specific materials. Cast aluminum cladding on the Palace side buildings in Tokyo (Fig. 6.5) exemplifies the delicate manufacturing processes that can be achieved and the complicated assembly work that needed to be accomplished to satisfy the high degree of precision demanded by this particular client.

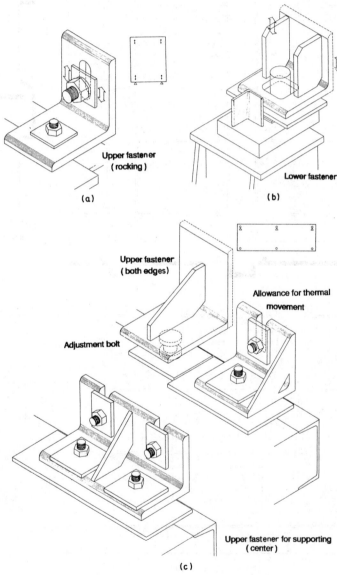

Fig. 6.4 Rocking mechanism in Tokyo IBM headquarters.

Construction details shown in Fig. 6.6 exemplify the craftsmanship of the workers who individually hand-manufactured the cast panels. A recent rise in the price of electricity has increased the cost for this type of system significantly and thus reduced its usage.

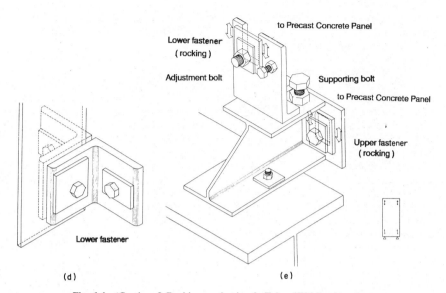

Fig. 6.4 *(Continued)* **Rocking mechanism in Tokyo IBM headquarters.**

(a)

Fig. 6.5 **Cast aluminum cladding on Palace side building.**

Having swept the globe, the industrial revolution has now been coupled with a new revolution in electronic technology. In Japan this coupling has manifested itself in the design of building maintenance robots. The maintenance of cladding systems is essential for extending the serviceable life span of a building skin. Window washing, resealing joints, and general surface cleaning and painting are often tedious and dangerous. Figure 6.7 shows two automatic cleaning machines that have been developed to reduce worker risk and increase the efficiency of exterior building maintenance.

As an alternative to using robots to rebuild cladding joints and relying on sealant selection and performance as described in Chapter 2, the Japanese are experimenting with open-joint waterproofing, a modification of the rain-screen principles developed in western countries. In this system (Fig. 6.8) a gasket is located deep within the cladding material joint and is protected by a brush that collects and diverts water. Diverted water is then channeled out of the cladding system through a series of open joints designed into the system (Fig. 6.9).

In a 1986 technical memorandum prepared for the Congress of the United States, the U.S. Office of Technology Assessment listed numerous ways in which developments in ceramics would begin to establish a new global technological direction for the design of everything from automobiles and computers to space modules. The Japanese are on the creative forefront with the introduction of a hollow extruded ceramic for exterior walls of multistory buildings. The boards are water repellent and are 450 mm (18 in.) wide by 5000 mm (20 in.) long by 55 or 65 mm (2 or 2.5 in.) thick.

(b)

Fig. 6.5 (*Continued*) **Cast aluminum cladding on Palace side building.**

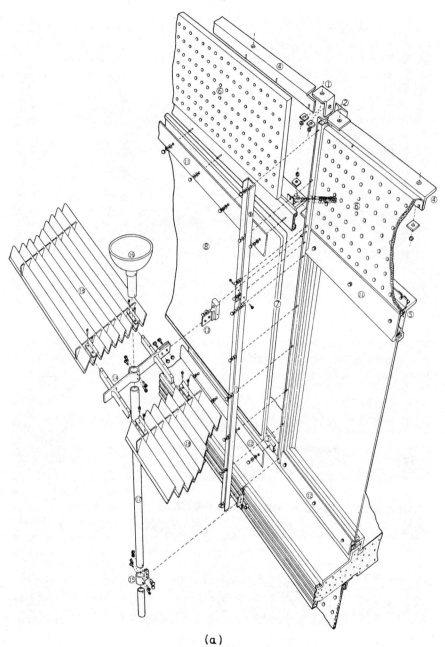

(a)

Fig. 6.6   Details in Palace side building.

(b)

(c)

Fig. 6.6   (*Continued*) Details in Palace side building.

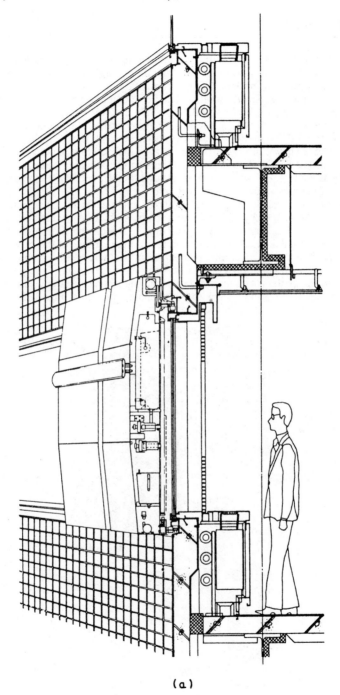

(a)

Fig. 6.7   Examples of window washing robots.

6.2 GERMANY

While Japan was developing aluminum casting techniques, Germany discovered opportunities afforded by sophisticated metal-bending technology. Working with metal manufacturers to understand and control the internal stresses inherent in a piece of manufactured sheet metal, at least one company has been able to fabricate large cladding panels of up to 2.13 by 5.79 m (7 by 19 ft) that do not rely on the sandwich panel technology used in other countries, thus eliminating the potential for panel delamination or deterioration. Several details of Pohl Europanel technology are shown in Figs. 6.10 and 6.11. This cladding panel system, developed by Christian Pohl GmbH, sets no limits to the designer's imagination. Panels can be large or small, with round or straight bends, and can be fabricated with a variety of stainless-steel finishes and colors.

In addition to metal cladding systems, glazed and unglazed ceramic panels having a maximum size of 1600 by 1250 by 8 mm (63 by 49 by 0.3 in.) thick are also being manufactured in Germany. One system incorporates a unique concealed attachment unit, whereby stainless-steel bolts are secured to the rear face of the panel in predetermined positions using a ceramic cup of exceptional strength fired onto the panel. The bolt and its ceramic housing then become an integral part of the panel, which forms a rain screen to protect insulation and the supporting substrate. The material is said to be self-cleaning and resistant to atmospheric pollution (Fig. 6.12).

(b)

Fig. 6.7 (*Continued*) **Examples of window washing robots.**

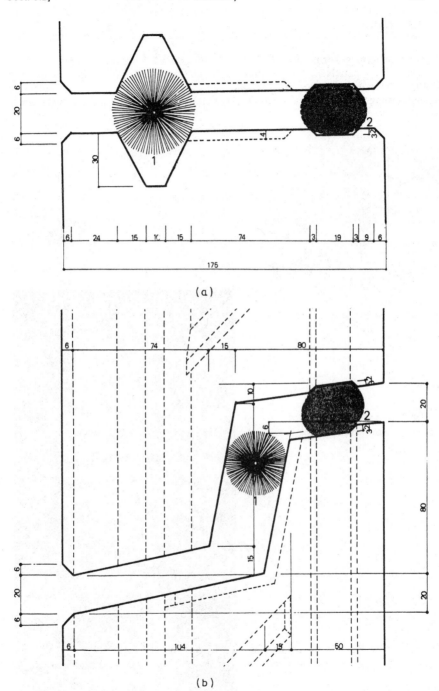

Fig. 6.8   Gasket and brush diverter.

6.3 ITALY

Tecnomaiera, a Turin-based firm, has developed a laminating process by which sawn stone panels can be laminated to an expanded steel reinforcing mesh through the use of epoxy and a unique vacuum chamber. The panels are currently undergoing wind load, flammability, weathering, and anchor-pullout tests under

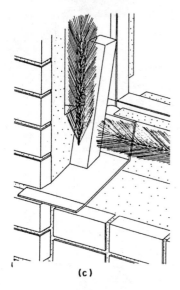

(c)

Fig. 6.8 *(Continued)* **Gasket and brush diverter.**

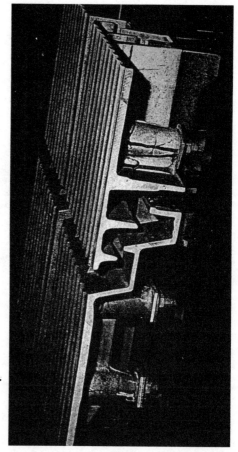

Fig. 6.9 Integral cladding drainage channels.

(a)

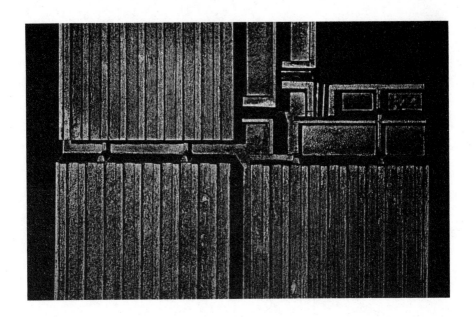

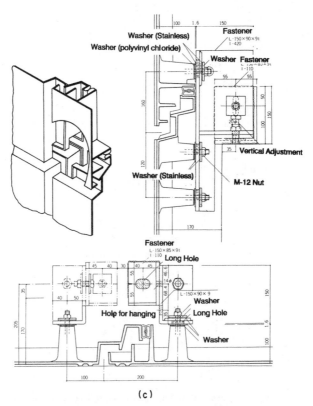

(c)

Fig. 6.9 (*Continued*) Integral cladding drainage channels.

115

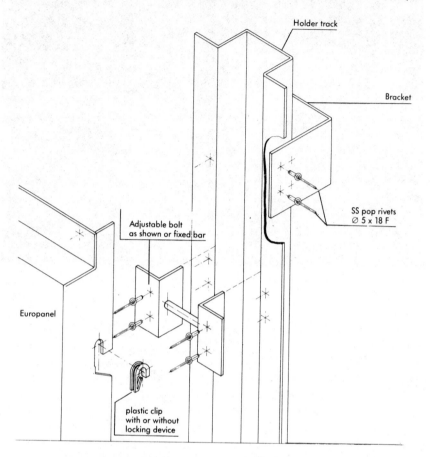

Holder track

Bracket

SS pop rivets
Ø 5 x 18 F

Adjustable bolt
as shown or fixed bar

Europanel

plastic clip
with or without
locking device

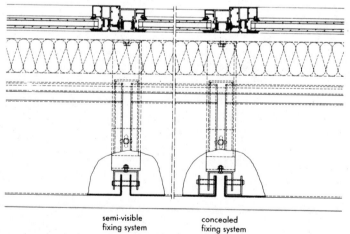

semi-visible
fixing system

concealed
fixing system

Fig. 6.10   Metal panel attachment and fixing systems. (Courtesy of Pohl Europanel.)

The technical details of a custom designed facade panel

Aluminium panel, constructed from 3 mm (.12 in.) sheets.

Color: baked enamel in color chart no. RAL 3003 in accordance with GSB specifications.

Panels are supported by channels which also serve to direkt water run-off.

Holding tracks and pins invisible.

1 Flashing
2 Insulation
3 Fasteners acc. to static requirements
4 Wall-anchor adjustable in 3 directions
5 Seropal – Sandwich Panel
6 Ceiling
7 Exterior Sunblind
8 Continuous window sill
9 3-mm Aluminium powder coated Panel with sound dampening
10 Continuous supporting channels designed to direct water run-off

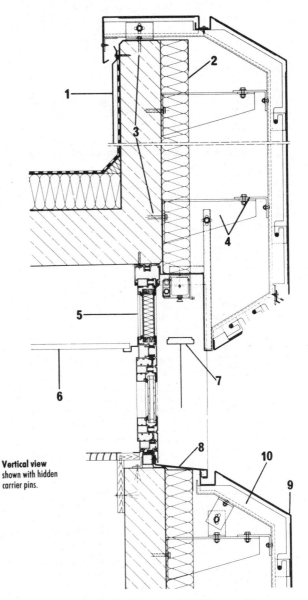

Vertical view shown with hidden carrier pins.

Fig. 6.11   Metal panel at window head and sill. (Courtesy of Pohl Europanel.)

ASTM criteria. Fabricated in sizes up to 1.52 by 3.04 m (5 by 10 ft), the 4.8-mm (3/16-in.) panels weigh only about 129 Pa (2.7 lb/ft^2).

6.4   UNITED STATES

Of 28 randomly selected tall buildings constructed throughout the United States in 1988 to 1990, 26 incorporated glass and granite cladding systems. Because of

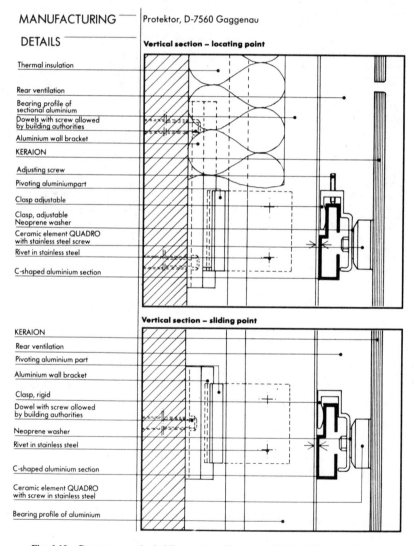

Fig. 6.12   German ceramic cladding system. (Courtesy of Buchtal Ceramic Works.)

the unpredictability of stone, as discussed in Chapter 5, it comes as no surprise that designers who want the look of stone are turning to new materials that offer similar color and texture but with predictable performance. Once again, ceramic materials seem to provide an alternative. Recently introduced into the United States, Neoparies is a Japanese exterior material made of crystallized glass that offers some of the esthetic and structural characteristics of stone without the weight. Manufactured by the Nippon Electric Glass Company, the material has a specific gravity of 2.7 g/cm^3 and has already captured about 20% of the Asian stone market. It was recently proposed as a replacement for the failing marble

Perspective

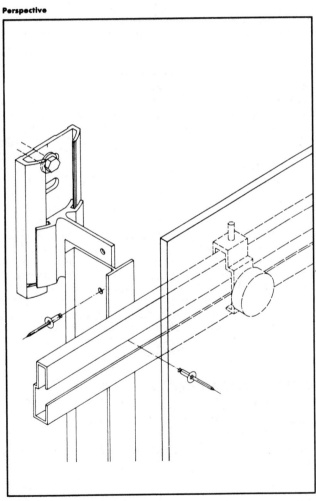

Fig. 6.12 (*Continued*)   German ceramic cladding system. (Courtesy of Buchtal Ceramic Works.)

cladding system on Chicago's Amoco building. The recladding proposal was rejected, however, in favor of a granite system.

Like the Japanese and the Germans, the Americans are also looking to ceramics as a means for cladding tall buildings. Researchers in the Center for Engineering Ceramic Manufacturing at Clemson University and the Department of Architecture at Iowa State University are investigating how the use of a lightweight cladding system (approximately 1.04 g/m^3) made of foamed clay with an impervious glass coating could affect the cost, quality, and performance of tall buildings.

6.5 RESEARCH NEEDS

In discussing the relationship between cladding system durability, its structural contribution, and building esthetics, two conditions seem to need further critical evaluation.

First, in what ways should the cladding system act as a complement to the major structural system in providing wind bracing and augmenting building stability? An analogy in structural performance can be drawn with the evolution of automobile design. In the early stages of their development, vehicles were designed with primary structural frames supporting fenders, doors, trunk lids, and such. Current technology relies on these same components to act as a unit body, with each component contributing to the structural integrity of the whole, eliminating the need for a separate primary framing structure. Is it possible, as it was with the automobile, to decrease weight, improve both internal structural performance and highway performance, and at the same time reduce construction costs?

The second point to be considered is the relationship between the functional and the esthetic life span of the cladding system. Cladding systems are exposed to very harsh environmental conditions that can contribute to the rapid aging of sealants and other system components. In addition, much of the building's visual image comes from the cladding. Should building owners, developers, and designers begin to focus on the design of systems that can be replaced or recycled in 30 to 40 years? If so, designers may have to begin developing a new palate of materials with which to design—those offering durability, recyclability, and imagability. Whatever the case, it seems that new technologies in materials and systems will ultimately have a profound impact on the tall-building built environment.

6.6 CONDENSED REFERENCES/BIBLIOGRAPHY

Bassler 1990, *Innovative Tall Building Design: An Integration of Materials and Systems*
Blatterman 1991, *Reinforced Stone Veneer*
Council on Tall Buildings, Group SC 1980, *Tall Building Systems and Concepts*
Solomon 1990, *Made in Japan*

Research Needs

The research issues that need to be addressed fall into the basic categories of:

1. Life safety
2. Visual appearance
3. Maintenance
4. Water/air resistance
5. Energy conservation

It is at times the case that problems, and therefore research needs, are often regional. For example, Los Angeles' seismic challenge in the design of cladding connections is not an issue in New York or London. However, in climates that experience vast temperature differentials, and brutal winters, building cladding research challenges include a whole array of energy conservation, water/air resistance, and maintenance issues.

In some instances, research is needed not just to solve a problem to which a solution already exists, but to find a way to solve a problem less expensively. For example, the industry standard thickness for stone veneer of cladding has become so thin that failure of these materials has in some cases become catastrophic. It is clear that this problem can be averted simply by going back to the old standard thickness of stone. However, the great expense of the stone makes it desirable to find a way to design with thinner veneer, yet avoid the predictable problems.

Some of the five categories listed overlap in specific problems, thus research solutions must be found that do not exacerbate one problem in the process of solving another. The researcher will most likely concentrate on a particular technical problem, pinpoint the dynamics or mechanics of the problem, and possibly address this unique problem in suggesting a solution. It is the practitioner who must be aware of the particular set of conditions and challenges facing the building being designed and consider whether and how a solution to a particular aspect of building performance will affect other aspects of the building.

For example, while larger joints between cladding elements help the building skin to accommodate interstory drift, these larger joints also pose a much more difficult problem in the proper sealing of joints between panels. The interstory drift that may result from an earthquake, thus the horrifying scenario of cladding panels raining down on pedestrians, is a potential, monumental life-safety issue. However, such a large quake may not even occur in the lifespan of the building, while the sealing of the building, though not a life-safety issue, is sure to become a maintenance, water/air resistance and energy conservation issue within a building's first year of occupancy.

Beyond the technical balance of finding solutions in applied research, are the practical considerations of economics, liability, and probability. In this context of balancing competing considerations by using judgment and experience, the design of and research in cladding issues is as much an art as it is engineering and science.

An issue in the research needs of many areas including the specific area of cladding for tall buildings, is a way to improve international communication. Distance and language barriers are unfortunate obstacles to the exchange of research findings. For example, while the Building Research Institute and various universities and construction companies in Japan have published and put into practice the results of a prodigious amount of research in cladding performance (ranging from seismic behavior, to joints and seals performance, to glass failure), almost none of this has gone beyond Japan. One reason is that few people outside Japan read Japanese; the other reason is that there are too few conduits through which exchange of ideas over long distances can take place. Perhaps not a research need, but a research related need, is improvement and augmentation of international exchange.

Nomenclature

Abrasion resistance. The ability of a material to withstand a wearing away caused by friction.

Acid environment. Circumstances or conditions surrounding a building that include any of a large class of substances whose aqueous solutions are capable of turning litmus indicators red and will react with and dissolve certain metals to form salts.

Acid rain. Acid precipitation falling as rain.

Acrylic. A group of thermoplastic resins formed by polymerizing the esters of acrylic acid.

Adhesive bonding. The ability of two dissimilar materials to stick to one another.

Admixtures. A substance other than cement, water, and aggregates included in a concrete mixture for the purpose of altering one or more properties of the concrete.

Air infiltration. The accidental influx of outside air due to air leakage through the building skin.

Alkaline environment. Circumstances or conditions surrounding a building that include a carbonate or hydroxide of an alkali metal, whose aqueous solution is bitter, slippery, caustic, and typically basic in reactions.

Anchor stresses. The mechanical pressure or force present at a point of support or attachment.

Anemometer. An instrument for indicating and measuring wind force and velocity.

Application life. The period of time during which a sealant, after being mixed with a catalyst or exposed to the atmosphere, remains suitable for application. Also referred to as work life.

Backer framing. A skeletal structure used to support a thin facing material.

Back-up material. A compressible material placed in a joint before applying a sealant, to limit the depth of the sealant and assist in providing the proper sealant configuration. This material may also act as a bond breaker. *See* Bond breaker.

Back-up wall. A vertical plane of masonry, concrete, or framing used to support a thin facing such as a single wythe of brickwork.

Batt insulation. Insulation in the form of a mass of fibers, usually available in standard widths to fit between joists and rafters.

Batten. A strip of wood or metal used to cover the crack between two adjoining panels.

Bead. A narrow line of sealant.

Beaded joint. A joint with a narrow convex profile.

Bearing connections. The point at which one building element rests on, and is attached to, another.

Bed. The bead of compound applied between sight bar glass or panel and the stationary stop or sight bar of the sash or frames, and usually the first bead of compound to be applied when setting glass or panels.

Bidding. Making an offer to perform a quantity of work or provide a quantity of material at a specified price.

Bite. The depth to which the edge of a piece of glass is held by its frame.

Blanket insulation. An enclosing layer of insulation.

Bleeding. A liquid coating or drops of a liquid component that migrate to the surface of a sealant.

Blind anchorages. A concealed point of attachment.

Block. A small piece of wood, lead, Neoprene, or other suitable material used to position the panel in the frame.

Bond failure. A condition of insufficient or inadequate adhesion.

Bond breaker. A strip of material to which sealant does not adhere.

Brick. A masonry unit approximating a rectangular prism in shape and made from burned clay, shale, or a mixture of both (a ceramic product).

Buckling failure. Structural failure by gross lateral deflection of a slender element under compressive stress.

Building envelope. The materials and structure that enclose the building, comparable in function to human skin.

Building facade. The face of a building.

Bulk compound. Sealants in containers or cartridges capable of being extruded in place.

Butted joint. A condition in which two materials are joined end to end with no mullion between them.

Butyl sealants. A synthetic rubber compound formed by the copolymerization of isobutylene with isoprene and used to prevent the penetration of water or air through a joint.

Caulking. The process of making a joint watertight. The term originally implied stopping up joints with oakum (loose fiber from old rope) and melted pitch. It is now also applied to stopping joints with lead, mastics, rubber, and other flexible materials.

Cavities. Continuous horizontal and vertical spaces between wythes of masonry walls and wythes tied together by metal ties.

Cement. Any of various construction adhesives, consisting of powdered, calcined rock and clay materials, that form a paste with water and can be molded or poured to set as a solid mass.

Ceramic. Any of various hard, brittle, heat- and corrosion-resistant materials made by shaping and then firing a nonmetallic mineral, as clay, at a high temperature.

Cladding. The exterior covering of the structural components of a building.

Clip angles. Miscellaneous sizes and shapes of metal used to attach cladding materials to subframes.

Cohesive failure. Splitting and opening of a compound resulting from overextension of the compound.

Compatibility. The ability of two or more materials to exist in close and permanent association for an indefinite period with no adverse effect of one on the other.

Conductivity. The ability or power to conduct or transmit.

Cure rate. The time frame in which a material is preserved or finished by a chemical or physical process.

Curtain wall. A building exterior wall, of any material, which carries no superimposed vertical loads.

Crystallized glass panels. A building material having a marblelike texture and produced by heating granular glass particles until they are fused together to form needle-shaped crystals.

Damping. The capacity built into a device to prevent excessive correction and the resulting instability or oscillatory conditions.

Davit. A small crane that projects over the side of a building, usually used to support the equipment and personnel responsible for cleaning the building exterior.

Deflection. Movement of a structure or structural part due to stress.

Deformation. A change in the shape of a structure or structural element caused by a load or force acting on the structure.

Design-construction firm. An organization that provides both design and construction services, but operates as a single-source of responsibility.

Dew point. The temperature at which air becomes saturated and produces dew.

Differential heat gain. Variations in the heat flow into a building or object.

Drift. Lateral deflection of a building due to wind or other loads.

Drift index. The ratio of lateral deflection to height.

Drywall. An interior facing panel consisting of a gypsum core sandwiched between paper faces. Also called *gypsum board, plasterboard.*

Ductility. The ability of structural elements or frames to absorb energy through deformation without failure.

Dynamic response time. The amount of time necessary for an object to be set in motion as a result of an applied force.

Eddies. Currents as of air or water, moving contrary to the direction of the main current.

EIFS. *See* Exterior insulation finish systems.

Elastic. Able to return to its original size and shape after removal of stress.

Elastomeric. Rubberlike.

Elongation. Stretching under load; growing longer because of temperature expansion.

Empirical design procedures. Design procedures which rely on information gained from experience or observation.

Environmental controls. Those systems used to manage or modify the climatic conditions within a building.

Exterior insulation finish systems (EIFS). A cladding system that consists of a thin layer of reinforced stucco applied directly to the surface of an insulating plastic foam board.

Facing brick. A brick selected on the basis of appearance and durability for use in the exposed surface of a wall.

Fenestration. The design and position of windows in a building.

Fiber-reinforced concrete (FRC). *See* Glass fiber-reinforced concrete.

Flashing. A thin continuous sheet of metal, plastic, rubber, or waterproof paper used to prevent the passage of water through a joint in a wall, roof, chimney, etc.

Flexure. An act or instance of bending.

Frame buckling. A condition under which a symmetrical frame subjected to symmetric loading may suddenly deflect in an unsymmetrical mode and be unable to carry any increase in load.

Frame creep. A gradual shift of the structural frame of a building.

FRC (fiber-reinforced concrete). *See* Glass fiber-reinforced concrete.

Galvanized. Treated with a zinc coating as a means of preventing corrosion, e.g., galvanized steel.

GFRC. *See* Glass-fiber reinforced concrete.

Girt frame system. A metal framing system consisting of primary and secondary members used to support a cladding material.

Glass block. A hollow masonry unit made of glass.

Glass fiber-reinforced concrete (GFRC). Concrete with a strengthening admixture of short alkali-resistant glass fibers.

Graded-aggregate. Inert particles such as sand, gravel, crushed stone, or expanded minerals that have been classified by size or quality to achieve a particular effect in a concrete mixture.

Granite. A common coarse-grained, light-colored, hard igneous rock consisting mostly of quartz, orthoclase or microcline, and mica, used in monuments and for building.

Gust pressure. A measure of the magnitude of a rush of wind.

Gusts. Violent, abrupt rushes of wind.

Gypsum board. *See* Drywall.

Hollow brick. A hollow clay masonry unit whose net cross-sectional area (solid area) in any plane parallel to the bearing surface is less than 75% of its gross cross-sectional area measured in the same plane.

Honed finish. A smooth finish on stone achieved by grinding the stone with an abrasive surface.

In-plane distortions. Shape irregularities occurring in any of the planes of a clay masonry unit.

Infiltration. Air flowing inward as through walls or cracks.

Initial rate of absorption. A measure of the amount of moisture that can be sucked into a clay masonry unit in a designated period of time.

Internal drainage. A system for gathering and transferring moisture that has accumulated within a wall system to the exterior of the wall.

Interstory drift. A measure of the difference in lateral displacement occurring between various floor levels of a building.

Joint. A point or position at which two or more things are joined.

Joint tooling. The finishing of a mortar joint or sealant joint by pressing and compacting it to create a particular profile.

Kerf. A groove or notch made by a cutting tool.

Knife consistency. Compound formulated in a degree of firmness suitable for application with a glazing knife such as is used for face glazing and other sealant applications.

Laminar flow. Nonturbulent flow of a viscous fluid in layers near a boundary.

Life cycle. A usable period of time.

Limestone. A sedimentary rock consisting of calcium carbonate, magnesium carbonate, or both.

Loadbearing. Supporting a superimposed weight or force.

Marble. A metamorphic rock formed from limestone by heat and pressure.

Masonry veneer. A single wythe of masonry used as a facing over a frame of wood or metal.

Mica. Any of a group of chemically and physically related mineral silicates, common in igneous and metamorphic rocks, that contain hydroxyl, alkali, and aluminum silicate groups and can be split into flexible sheets used in insulation.

Migration. Spreading or creeping of a constituent of a compound onto adjacent surfaces.

Modulus of elasticity. The ratio of the direct stress of a linearly elastic material to its strain, also called Young's modulus.

Mullions. Vertical or horizontal bars between adjacent window or door units.

Nonsag (sealant). A sealant formulation having a consistency that will permit application in vertical joints without appreciable sagging or slumping.

Nonskinning. Descriptive of a product that does not form a surface skin.

Nonstaining. Characteristic of a compound that will not stain a surface.

Oxidizing. The process of corroding or rusting.

Parapet. The region of an exterior wall that projects above the level of the roof.

Peel test. The separation of a bond, whereby the material is pulled away from the mating surface at a 90° angle or a 180° angle to the plane to which it is adhered. Values are generally expressed in pounds per inch width and as to whether failure was adhesive or cohesive.

Perm. A unit of vapor permeability.

Permeability. The rate of diffusion of a pressurized gas through a porous material.

Plasterboard. *See* Drywall.

Plastics. Synthetically produced giant molecules.

Polyethylene. A thermoplastic widely used in sheet form for vapor retarders, moisture barriers, and temporary construction coverings.

Polymer. A large molecule composed of many identical chemical units.

Polysulfide. A high-range gunnable sealant.

Portland cement. The gray powder used as the binder in concrete, mortar, and stucco.

Polyurethane. Any of a large group of resins and synthetic rubber compounds used in sealants, varnishes, insulating foams, and roof membranes.

Prefabricate. A term applied to structural elements or components which are built at a remote location, usually a factory, and then transported to the site and erected.

Pressure taps. Points at which pressure is measured.

Primers. A coating that prepares a surface to receive another type of coating or sealant.

Raked joint. A masonry joint in which the mortar is recessed from the exterior plane of the wall, emphasizing the pattern of masonry while deemphasizing the mortar.

Rocking connections. A complex connection, developed by the Japanese, for the attachment of cladding systems to the structural frame of a building.

Safing. Fire-resistant material inserted into a space between a curtain wall and a spandrel beam or column, to retard the passage of fire through the space.

Sandwich panels. A panel consisting of two outer faces of wood, metal, gypsum, or concrete bonded to a core of insulating foam or other dissimilar material.

Sash. Framework holding the glass and glazing system.

Saturation coefficient. Used in determining the durability of clay masonry, it is the ratio of the 24-hour cold water absorption divided by the 5-hour boiling absorption.

Sealant discoloration. The migration of certain chemicals within a sealant that results in the changing of the natural color of the surrounding materials.

Sealants. Materials used to exclude water and solid foreign matter from joints. [*See also* Butyl sealants; Nonsag (sealant); Two-part sealants.]

Seismic loads. Forces on a building resulting from an earthquake or earth tremor.

Shear. A condition caused by forces that tend to produce an opposite but parallel sliding motion of the body's planes.

Shelf angle. A steel angle attached to the spandrel of a building to support a masonry facing.

Sidesway. The lateral movement of a structure under the action of lateral loads, unsymmetrical vertical loads, or unsymmetrical properties of the structure.

Silicone. A polymer used for high-range sealants, roof membranes, and masonry water repellants.

Sill. The horizontal bottom portion of a window or door.

Slate. A metamorphic form of clay, easily split into thin sheets.

Sound transmission class (STC). An index of the resistance of a partition or ceiling to the passage of sound.

Spandrel. The wall area between the head of a window on one story and the sill of a window on the floor above.

STC. *See* Sound transmission class.

Story drift. The lateral displacement of an individual story of a building under load.

Stress. Force per unit area.

Structural glazing. Glass secured to the face of a building with strong, highly adhesive silicone sealant so as to eliminate the need for any metal to appear outside the inner face of the glass.

Stucco. Portland cement plaster used as an exterior cladding or siding material.

Tempered glass. Glass that has been heat-treated to increase its toughness and its resistance to breakage.

Tensile strength. The ability of a structural material to withstand stretching forces.

Thermoplastic. Having the property of softening when heated and rehardening when cooled.

Thin stone veneer. Stone veneer that is 50 mm or less in thickness.

Travertine. A richly patterned marblelike form of limestone.

Turbulence. Airflow having local velocities and pressures that fluctuate randomly.

Two-part sealants. Sealants consisting of an agent and a catalyst which must be mixed together prior to application.

Unbonded stone veneer. A system in which the stone is not grouted or bonded to the surrounding material.

Underwriters Laboratories. An organization whose testing and certification program exerts a major influence on construction standards.

Urethane. A colorless crystalline or white granular compound used as a solvent.

Velocity. A vector quantity whose magnitude is a body's speed and whose direction is the body's direction of motion.

Veneer. *See* Masonry veneer; Thin stone veneer; Unbonded stone veneer.

Vulcanize. To increase the strength, resiliency, and freedom from stickiness and odor by combining with sulfur or other additives in the presence of heat and pressure (e.g., rubber).

Water-cement ratio. A numerical index of the relative proportions of water and cement in a concrete mixture.

Weathered joint. A mortar joint finished in a sloping, planar profile that tends to shed water to the outside of the wall.

Weathering. The change of properties and constituents of a material caused by the effects of heat, water, chemicals, freezing, and other similar factors.

Weephole. A small opening whose purpose is to permit drainage of water that accumulates inside a building component.

Wetting. Causing a liquid to penetrate into the surface of a solid.

Wind loading. The force exerted on the exterior of a building by the wind.

Wind tunnel. A chamber through which air is forced at controllable velocities in order to study the aerodynamic flow around and effects on objects, airfoils, or scale models, mounted within.

Work life. *See* Application life.

Young's modulus. *See* Modulus of elasticity.

ABBREVIATIONS

AAMA   Architectural Aluminum Manufacturers Association
ACI   American Concrete Institute
AIJ   Architectural Institute of Japan
AISI   American Iron and Steel Institute
ANSI   American National Standards Institute
ASTM   American Society for Testing and Materials
BIA   Brick Institute of America
BOCA   Building Officials and Code Administrators International
ICBO   International Conference of Building Officials
NAAMM   National Association of Architectural Metal Manufacturers
PCI   Prestressed Concrete Institute
PPG   Pittsburgh Plate Glass
SBCCI   Southern Building Code Congress International
UL   Underwriters Laboratories

UNITS

In the table below are given conversion factors for commonly used units. The numerical values have been rounded off to the values shown. The British (Imperial) System of units is the same as the American System except where noted. Le Système International d'Unités (abbreviated "SI") is the name formally given in 1960 to the system of units partly derived from, and replacing, the old metric system.

SI	American	Old metric
	Length	
1 mm	0.03937 in.	1 mm
1 m	3.28083 ft	1 m
	1.093613 yd	
1 km	0.62137 mile	1 km
	Area	
1 mm^2	0.00155 in.^{2}	1 mm^2
1 m^2	10.76392 ft^2	1 m^2
	1.19599 yd^2	
1 km^2	247.1043 acres	1 km^2
1 hectare	2.471 acres[1]	1 hectare
	Volume	
1 cm^3	0.061023 in.^{3}	1 cc
		1 ml
1 m^3	35.3147 ft^3	1 m^3
	1.30795 yd^3	
	264.172 gal[2] liquid	
	Velocity	
1 m/sec	3.28084 ft/sec	1 m/sec
1 km/hr	0.62137 miles/hr	1 km/hr
	Acceleration	
1 m/sec^2	3.28084 ft/sec^2	1 m/sec^2
	Mass	
1 g	0.035274 oz	1 g

SI	American	Old metric
1 kg	2.2046216 lb[3]	1 kg
	Density	
1 kg/m^3	0.062428 lb/ft^3	1 kg/m^3
	Force, Weight	
1 N	0.224809 lbf	0.101972 kgf
1 kN	0.1124045 tons[4]	
1 MN	224.809 kips	
1 kN/m	0.06853 kips/ft	
1 kN/m^2	20.9 lbf/ft^2	
	Torque, Bending Moment	
1 N-m	0.73756 lbf-ft	0.101972 kgf-m
1 kN-m	0.73756 kip-ft	101.972 kgf-m
	Pressure, Stress	
1 N/m^2 = 1 Pa	0.000145038 psi	0.101972 kgf/m^2
1 kN/m^2 = 1 kPa	20.8855 psf	
1 MN/m^2 = 1 MPa	0.145038 ksi	
	Viscosity (Dynamic)	
1 N-sec/m^2	0.0208854 lbf-sec/ft^2	0.101972 kgf-sec/m^2
	Viscosity (Kinematic)	
1 m^2/sec	10.7639 ft^2/sec	1 m^2/sec
	Energy, Work	
1 J = 1 N-m	0.737562 lbf-ft	0.00027778 w-hr
1 MJ	0.37251 hp-hr	0.27778 kw-hr
	Power	
1 W = 1 J/sec	0.737562 lbf ft/sec	1 w
1 kW	1.34102 hp	1 kw
	Temperature	
K = 273.15 + °C	°F = (°C × 1.8) + 32	°C = (°F − 32)/1.8
K = 273.15 + 5/9(°F − 32)		
K = 273.15 + 5/9(°R − 491.69)		

(1)Hectare as an alternative for km^2 is restricted to land and water areas.
(2)1 m^3 = 219.9693 Imperial gallons.
(3)1 kg = 0.068522 slugs.
(4)1 American ton = 2000 lb.   1 kN = 0.1003612 Imperial ton.   1 Imperial ton = 2240 lb.

Abbreviations for Units

Btu	British thermal unit	kW	kilowatt
°C	degree Celsius (centigrade)	lb	pound
cc	cubic centimeters	lbf	pound force
cm	centimeter	lb_m	pound mass
°F	degree Fahrenheit	MJ	megajoule
ft	foot	MPa	megapascal
g	gram	m	meter
gal	gallon	ml	milliliter
hp	horsepower	mm	millimeter
hr	hour	MN	meganewton
Imp	British Imperial	N	newton
in.	inch	oz	ounce
J	joule	Pa	pascal
K	Kelvin	psf	pounds per square foot
kg	kilogram	psi	pounds per square inch
kgf	kilogram-force	°R	degree Rankine
kip	1000 pound force	sec	second
km	kilometer	slug	14.594 kg
kN	kilonewton	U_o	heat transfer coefficient
kPa	kilopascal	W	watt
ksi	kips per square inch	yd	yard

References/Bibliography

The citations that follow include both references and bibliography. The list includes all articles referred to or cited in the text and also includes bibliography for further reading. The material is arranged alphabetically by author.

American Concrete Institute Committee 381, 1989
BUILDING CODE REQUIREMENTS FOR REINFORCED CONCRETE, ACI 318, American Concrete Institute, Detroit, Mich.

American Concrete Institute Committee 530, 1988
SPECIFICATION FOR MASONRY STRUCTURES, ACI 530/ASCE 5, American Concrete Institute, Detroit, Michigan, and American Society of Civil Engineers, New York

American Concrete Institute Committee 533, 1965
PRECAST CONCRETE WALL PANELS, ACI 533, American Concrete Institute, Detroit, Mich.

American Concrete Institute Committee 544, 1982
STATE-OF-THE-ART REPORT ON FIBER REINFORCED CONCRETE, ACI 544.1, American Concrete Institute, Detroi, Mich.

American Insurance Association, 1976
NATIONAL BUILDING CODE, American Insurance Association, New York

American Iron and Steel Institute, 1980
SPECIFICATION FOR THE DESIGN OF COLD-ROLLED FORMED STRUCTURAL MEMBERS, American Iron and Steel Institute, Washington, D.C.

American National Standards Institute, 1953
AMERICAN STANDARD BUILDING CODE REQUIREMENTS FOR MASONRY, ANSI A41.1, American National Standards Institute, New York

American National Standards Institute, 1982
AMERICAN NATIONAL STANDARD MINIMUM DESIGN LOADS FOR BUILDINGS AND OTHER STRUCTURES, ANSI A58.1, American National Standards Institute, New York

American National Standards Institute, 1987
SAFETY PERFORMANCE SPECIFICATION AND METHOD OF TEST FOR SAFETY GLAZING MATERIALS USED IN BUILDINGS, ANSI Z97.1, American National Standards Institute, New York

American Society of Civil Engineers, 1988
PUBLICATION ON THE MINIMUM DESIGN LOADS FOR BUILDINGS AND OTHER STRUCTURES, ASCE, 7–88, New York.

American Society for Testing and Materials, 1988
SPECIFICATIONS FOR SEALED INSULATING GLASS UNITS, ASTM E 774, Committee E-6, American Society for Testing and Materials, Philadelphia, Pa.

American Society for Testing and Materials, 1985
STANDARD SPECIFICATION FOR CONCRETE BUILDING BRICK, ASTM C 55, Committee C-15, American Society for Testing and Materials, Philadelphia, Pa.

American Society for Testing and Materials, 1989
BUILDING BRICK (SOLID MASONRY UNITS MADE FROM CLAY OR SHALE),
ASTM C 62, Committee C-15, American Society for Testing and Materials, Philadelphia, Pa.

American Society for Testing and Materials, 1990
STANDARD TEST METHODS OF SAMPLING AND TESTING BRICK AND
STRUCTURAL CLAY TILE, ASTM C 67, American Society for Testing and Materials,
Philadelphia, Pa.

American Society for Testing and Materials, 1985
STANDARD SPECIFICATION FOR HOLLOW LOAD-BEARING CONCRETE MA-
SONRY UNITS, ASTM C 90, Committee C-15, American Society for Testing and Ma-
terials, Philadelphia, Pa.

American Society for Testing and Materials, 1986
CERAMIC GLAZED STRUCTURAL CLAY FACING TILE, FACING BRICK, AND
SOLID MASONRY UNITS, ASTM C 126, Committee C-15, American Society for Test-
ing and Materials, Philadelphia, Pa.

American Society for Testing and Materials, 1990
STANDARD METHODS OF SAMPLING AND TESTING CONCRETE MASONRY
UNITS, ASTM C 140, American Society for Testing and Materials, Philadelphia, Pa.

American Society for Testing and Materials, 1985
STANDARD SPECIFICATION FOR SOLID LOAD-BEARING CONCRETE MA-
SONRY UNITS, ASTM C 145, Committee C-15, American Society for Testing and Ma-
terials, Philadelphia, Pa.

American Society for Testing and Materials, 1989
FACING BRICK (SOLID MASONRY UNITS MADE FROM CLAY OR SHALE),
ASTM C 216, Committee C-15, American Society for Testing and Materials, Philadel-
phia, Pa.

American Society for Testing and Materials, 1988
STANDARD TEST METHOD FOR STEADY-STATE THERMAL PERFORMANCE
OF BUILDING ASSEMBLIES BY MEANS OF A GUARDED HOT BOX, ASTM C
236, American Society for Testing and Materials, Philadelphia, Pa.

American Society for Testing and Materials, 1989
STANDARD SPECIFICATION FOR MORTAR FOR UNIT MASONRY, ASTM C 270,
Committee C-12, American Society for Testing and Materials, Philadelphia, Pa.

American Society for Testing and Materials, 1990
STANDARD PRACTICE FOR MICROSCOPICAL DETERMINATION OF AIR-VOID
CONTENT AND PARAMETERS OF THE AIR-VOID SYSTEM IN HARDENED
CONCRETE, ASTM C 457, American Society for Testing and Materials, Philadelphia,
Pa.

American Society for Testing and Materials, 1983
STANDARD SPECIFICATION FOR GROUT FOR MASONRY, Committee C-12,
ASTM C 476, American Society for Testing and Materials, Philadelphia, Pa.

American Society for Testing and Materials, 1985
STANDARD SPECIFICATION FOR MARBLE BUILDING STONE (EXTERIOR),
ASTM C 503, Committee C-18, American Society for Testing and Materials, Philadel-
phia, Pa.

American Society for Testing and Materials, 1985
STANDARD SPECIFICATION FOR LIMESTONE BUILDING STONE, ASTM C 568,
Committee C-18, American Society for Testing and Materials, Philadelphia, Pa.

American Society for Testing and Materials, 1985
STANDARD SPECIFICATION FOR GRANITE BUILDING STONE, ASTM C 615,
Committee C-18, American Society for Testing and Materials, Philadelphia, Pa.

American Society for Testing and Materials, 1985
STANDARD SPECIFICATION FOR SANDSTONE BUILDING STONE, ASTM C 616,
Committee C-18, American Society for Testing and Materials, Philadelphia, Pa.

American Society for Testing and Materials, 1985
STANDARD SPECIFICATION FOR SLATE BUILDING STONE, ASTM C 629, Committee C-18, American Society for Testing and Materials, Philadelphia, Pa.

American Society for Testing and Materials, 1986
TEST METHOD FOR ADHESION AND COHESION OF ELASTOMERIC JOINT SEALANTS UNDER CYCLIC MOVEMENT, ASTM C 719, Committee C-24, American Society for Testing and Materials, Philadelphia, Pa.

American Society for Testing and Materials, 1990
STANDARD TEST METHOD FOR PRECONSTRUCTION AND CONSTRUCTION EVALUATION OF MORTARS FOR PLAIN AND REINFORCED UNIT MASONRY, ASTM C 780, American Society for Testing and Materials, Philadelphia, Pa.

American Society for Testing and Materials, 1990
STANDARD TEST METHOD FOR ADHESION-IN-PEEL OF ELASTOMERIC JOINT SEALANTS, ASTM C 794, American Society for Testing and Materials, Philadelphia, Pa.

American Society for Testing and Materials, 1986
GUIDE FOR USE OF ELASTOMERIC JOINT SEALANTS, ASTM C 962, American Society for Testing and Materials, Philadelphia, Pa.

American Society for Testing and Materials, 1990
TEST METHOD FOR THERMAL PERFORMANCES OF BUILDING ASSEMBLIES BY MEANS OF A CALIBRATED HOT BOX, ASTM C 976, American Society for Testing and Materials, Philadelphia, Pa.

American Society for Testing and Materials, 1990
STANDARD METHODS OF CONDUCTING STRENGTH TESTS OF PANELS FOR BUILDING CONSTRUCTION, ASTM E 72, American Society for Testing and Materials, Philadelphia, Pa.

American Society for Testing and Materials, 1990
STANDARD TEST METHOD FOR RATE OF AIR LEAKAGE THROUGH EXTERIOR WINDOWS, CURTAIN WALLS, AND DOORS, ASTM E 283, American Society for Testing and Materials, Philadelphia, Pa.

American Society for Testing and Materials, 1990
STANDARD TEST METHOD FOR STRUCTURAL PERFORMANCE OF EXTERIOR WINDOWS, CURTAIN WALLS, AND DOORS BY UNIFORM STATIC AIR PRESSURE DIFFERENCE, ASTM E 330, American Society for Testing and Materials, Philadelphia, Pa.

American Society for Testing and Materials, 1990
STANDARD TEST METHOD FOR WATER PENETRATION OF EXTERIOR WINDOWS, CURTAIN WALLS AND DOORS BY UNIFORM STATIC AIR PRESSURE DIFFERENCE, ASTM E 331, American Society for Testing and Materials, Philadelphia, Pa.

American Society for Testing and Materials, 1990
STANDARD TEST METHOD FOR WATER PENETRATION AND LEAKAGE THROUGH MASONRY, ASTM E 514, American Society for Testing and Materials, Philadelphia, Pa.

American Society for Testing and Materials, 1990
STANDARD TEST METHODS FOR FLEXURAL BOND STRENGTH OF MASONRY, ASTM E 518, American Society for Testing and Materials, Philadelphia, Pa.

American Society for Testing and Materials, 1990
STANDARD METHOD FOR FIELD MEASUREMENT OF AIR LEAKAGE THROUGH INSTALLED EXTERIOR WINDOWS AND DOORS, ASTM E 783, American Society for Testing and Materials, Philadelphia, Pa.

Architectural Aluminum Manufacturers Association, 1987a
ALUMINUM CURTAIN WALL DESIGN MANUAL, AAMA, Architectural Aluminum Manufacturers Association, Chicago, Ill.

Architectural Aluminum Manufacturers Association, 1987b
GUIDE SPECIFICATIONS MANUAL, AAMA, Architectural Aluminum Manufacturers Association, Chicago, Ill.

Architectural Aluminum Manufacturers Association, 1987c
VOLUNTARY SPECIFICATIONS FOR ALUMINUM PRIME WINDOWS, AAMA, Architectural Aluminum Manufacturers Association, Chicago, Ill.

Architectural Institute of Japan, 1985
RECOMMENDATIONS FOR ASEISMIC DESIGN AND CONSTRUCTION OF NONSTRUCTURAL ELEMENTS, Architectural Institute of Japan, Tokyo

Arumala, J. O., et al. 1982
PERFORMANCE EVALUATION OF BRICK VENEER WITH STEEL STUD BACKUP, Brick Institute of America and Metal Lath/Steel Framing Association, Clemson, S.C., April.

Asia Pacific Symposium on Wind Engineering, 1989
PROCEEDINGS ON RECENT ADVANCES IN WIND ENGINEERING, edited by T. F. Sun, Beijing, Pergamon, New York

Bassler, B. L., 1990
INNOVATIVE TALL BUILDING DESIGN: AN INTEGRATION OF MATERIALS AND SYSTEMS FROM OTHER DESIGN DISCIPLINES, *Proceedings from the 4th World Congress on Tall Buildings,* The Council on Tall Buildings and Urban Habitat, Hong Kong

Blatterman, J. F., 1991
REINFORCED STONE VENEER, *Architectural Record,* vol. 179, no. 2, February

Bonomo, F., 1988
UNA PELLE PROTETTIVA PER EDIFICI (PROTECTIVE SKIN FOR BUILDINGS), *L'Arca,* no. 16, pp. 86–87, May

Bordenaro, M. J., 1989
THIN STONE FACADES REVEAL VARIETY BUT CLOAK PROBLEMS, *Building Design and Construction,* vol. 30, no. 10, pp. 60–62

Bouwkamp, J. G., 1961
BEHAVIOR OF WINDOW PANELS UNDER IN-PLANE FORCE, *Bulletin of the Seismological Society of America,* vol. 51, no. 1, pp. 85–109, January

Brick Institute of America, 1969
RECOMMENDED PRACTICE FOR ENGINEERED BRICK MASONRY, Brick Institute of America, Reston, Va., February

Brick Institute of America, 1969
BUILDING CODE REQUIREMENTS FOR ENGINEERED BRICK MASONRY, Brick Institute of America, Reston, Va., February

Brick Institute of America, 1987
BRICK VENEER STEEL STUD WALLS, Technical Note no. 28B revised II, Brick Institute of America, Reston, Va., February

Brick Institute of America, 1987
STANDARD SPECIFICAITONS FOR PORTLAND CEMENT-LIME MORTAR FOR BRICK MASONRY, Brickf Insitute of America, Reston, Va.

Brooks, A., 1985
CONCEPTS IN CLADDING: CASE STUDIES OF JOINTING FOR ARCHITECTS AND ENGINEERS, Construction Press, London and New York

Brooks, A., 1988
OVERCLADDING: AN UNCERTAIN PANACEA, *Architects' Journal,* vol. 187, no. 4, pp. 67–69, January 27

Brooks, A., 1990
THE BUILDING ENVELOPE: APPLICATIONS OF NEW TECHNOLOGY CLADDING, Butterworths, London and Boston

Building, 1988
CLADDING AND CURTAINWALLING, *Building,* vol. 253, no. 17, pp. 3–57, April 22

Building Design, 1989
THROUGH A GLASS LIGHTLY, *Building Design,* pp. 14–15, July

Building Officials and Code Administrators International, 1990
BASIC BUILDING CODE, Building Officials and Code Administrators International, Inc., Homewood, Ill.

Campiono, A., 1988
IL RIVESTIMENTO LAPIDEO (STONE CLADDING), *Anfione Zeto,* vol. 1, no. 0, pp. 119–162

Cermak, J. E., 1971
LABORATORY SIMULATION OF THE ATMOSPHERIC BOUNDARY LAYER, *AIAA Journal,* vol. 9, September

Cermak, J. E., 1975
APPLICATIONS OF FLUID MECHANICS TO WIND ENGINEERING, a Freeman Scholar Lecture, *ASME Journal of Fluids Engineering,* vol. 97, no. 1, March

Cermak, J. E., 1979
WIND ENGINEERING, vols. 1 and 2, Pergamon, New York

Council on Tall Buildings, Group CL, 1980
TALL BUILDING CRITERIA AND LOADING, vol. CL, *Monograph on Planning and Design of Tall Buildings,* American Society of Civil Engineers, New York

Council on Tall Buildings, Group SB, 1979
STRUCTURAL DESIGN OF TALL STEEL BUILDINGS, vol. SB, *Monograph on Planning and Design of Tall Buildings,* American Society of Civil Engineers, New York

Davenport, A. G., 1960
WIND LOADS ON STRUCTURES, National Research Council of Canada, Division of Building Research, Ottawa, Ont., March

Davenport, A. G., 1967
GUST LOADING FACTORS, ASCE, *Journal of the Structural Division,* vol. 93, no. ST3, June

Davenport, A. G., 1961
THE APPLICATION OF STATISTICAL CONCEPTS TO THE WIND LOADING OF STRUCTURES, *Proceedings of the Institute of Civil Engineers,* vol. 19, August

Domus, 1986
UNA FACCIATA IN MATTONI, *Domus,* no. 678, pp. 8–10, December

Farinas, O., 1989
TODAY'S CLADDING MATERIALS, *Canadian Architect,* vol. 34, no. 10, pp. 71, 75, October

Fehlhaber, J. M., 1989
MEHR ALS VERPACKUNG: FASSADEN AUS BETON-FERTIGTEILEN—EINE STANDORTBESTIMMUNG, *Deutsches Architektenblatt,* vol. 21, pp. 507–512, April

Float Glass Marketing Association, 1989
GLAZING MANUAL, Float Glass Marketing Association (FGMA), Topeka, Kans.

Freedman, S., et al., 1989
ARCHITECTURAL PRECAST CONCRETE, 2d ed., Prestressed Concrete Institute, Chicago, Ill.

Gallagher, T., 1988
A VARIETY OF OPTIONS, *Plan: Architecture + Interior Design in Ireland,* vol. 19, no. 3, pp. 27–28, March

Gere, A. S., 1989
REPAIR OF EXTERIOR STONE ON HIGH-RISE BUILDINGS, *Building Stone Magazine,* no. 11–12, pp. 37–40, November–December

Goodno, B. J., et al., 1983
CLADDING STRUCTURE INTERACTION IN HIGHRISE BUILDINGS, Final Project Report, NSF Grant CEE 77042269, Atlanta, Ga.

Habasi, L., 1977
THE OBELISKS OF EGYPT; SKYSCRAPERS OF THE PAST, Scribner, New York

Harris, R. J., 1972
MEASUREMENTS OF WIND STRUCTURE, Symposium on Wind Loading on Structures, Bristol, June

Huls, M. E., 1985
CLADDING: A BIBLIOGRAPHY, Vance Bibliographies, Monticello, Ill.

Indiana Limestone Institute of America, 1984
INDIANA LIMESTONE HANDBOOK, 18th ed., Indiana Limestone Institute of America, Inc., Bedford, Ind.

International Conference of Building Officials, 1988
UNIFORM BUILDING CODE, International Conference of Building Officials, Whittier, Calif.

Jones, N., 1989
GREENHOUSE EFFECT, *Building Design,* pp. 5–7, March

Jones, N., 1989
TIME AND AGAIN, *Building Design,* pp. 18–19, March

Joscy, B., 1988
CURTAINWALLING AND LIGHT CLADDING, *RIBA Journal,* vol. 95, no. 7, pp. 63–83, July

Kent, C., 1989
AMOCO'S BLEMISHED SKIN, *Inland Architect,* vol. 33, no. 3, pp. 18–20, May–June

King, C., 1989
WAILING INNOVATION, *Building Design,* p. 28, Mar.

Klosowski, J. M., 1989
SEALANTS IN CONSTRUCTION, Marcel Dekker, New York

Knowles, E., et al., 1987
RECOMMENDED PRACTICE FOR GLASS FIBER REINFORCED CONCRETE PANELS, Precast/Prestressed Concrete Institute, Chicago, Ill.

Lawson, T. V., 1980
WIND EFFECTS ON BUILDINGS, vols. 1 and 2, Applied Science Publishers, London

Maile, R., 1986
CURTAINS UP!, *Building,* vol. 251, no. 40, pp. 27–28, October 3

Marble Institute of America, 1989
MARBLE INSTITUTE OF AMERICA MANUAL, The Marble Institute of America, Farmington, Mich.

Marcheso, E., 1989
AMOCO'S CARRARA SKIN TO BE REPLACED WITH GRANITE, *Architecture,* vol. 78, p. 26, October

Marsh, P., 1987
GETTING CONCRETE RIGHT...THE TECHNICAL SOPHISTICATION OF CONTEMPORARY PRECAST CLADDINGS, *Building Design,* no. 861, pp. 82–83, November 13

Masonry Advisory Council, 1987
DESIGN ALERTS, Masonry Advisory Council, Park Ridge, Ill.

McGuinness, T., 1989
CREATIVE DESIGN IN EXTERNAL METAL WALL CLADDING, *Plan: Architecture + Interior Design in Ireland,* vol. 20, no. 3, pp. 32–35, March

McGuire, P., 1989
PRODUCTS SURVEY: BUILDING WITH GLASS, *Architectural Review,* vol. 185, no.
1106, pp. 94–110, April

McGuire, P., 1989
PRODUCTS SURVEY: CLADDING, *Architectural Review,* vol. 186, no. 1114, pp. 90,
92, 96, 100, 102, 103, December

Mehta, J. B., 1978
HIGH-RISE BUILDINGS, Author, Bombay, India

Middle East Construction, 1986
CLADDING INNOVATIONS, *Middle East Construction,* vol. 11, no. 6, pp. 47, 49, 51,
June

Milton, H. J., 1990
INTERNATIONAL AND NATIONAL STANDARDS ON DIMENSIONAL COORDI-
NATION, MODULAR COORDINATION, TOLERANCES AND JOINTS IN BUILD-
ING, U.S. Dept. of Commerce, National Bureau of Standards

Ministry of Construction, 1989
JAPANESE NATIONAL BUILDING CODE, Ministry of Construction, Tokyo.

National Association of Architectural Metal Manufacturers, 1978
METAL CURTAIN WALL MANUAL, National Association of Architectural Metal
Manufacturers, Chicago, Ill.

National Building Quarries Association, 1984
SPECIFICATIONS FOR ARCHITECTURAL GRANITE, National Building Quarries
Association, Inc., Barre, Vt.

Owens-Corning Fiberglas Corporation, 1986
DESIGNING WITH FRC MATERIALS, Owens-Corning Fiberglas Corporation, Toledo,
Ohio

Pennsylvania State Producers Guild, 1983
SPECIFICATIONS FOR EXTERIOR STRUCTURAL SLATE, The Pennsylvania Slate
Producers Guild, Pen Argyl, Pa.

Penwarden, A. D., and Wise, A. F. E., 1975
WIND ENVIRONMENT AROUND BUILDINGS, Building Research Establishment Report, HMSO, London

Peterka, J. A., 1983
SELECTION OF LOCAL PEAK PRESSURE COEFFICIENTS FOR WIND TUNNEL
STUDIES OF BUILDINGS, 6th International Conference on Wind Engineering, Gold
Coast, Australia, March 21–25, CEP82-83, JAP9

Peterka, J. A., and Cermak, J. E., 1974
PEAK-PRESSURE DURATION IN SEPARATED REGIONS ON A STRUCTURE,
U.S.-Japan Seminar on Wind Effects on Structures, Kyoto, Japan, September 9–13,
1974; Report CEP 74-75JAP-JEC8, Fluid Mechanics Program, Colorado State University

PPG 1979
PPG THICKNESS RECOMMENDATIONS TO MEET ARCHITECTS SPECIFIED
ONE-MINUTE WIND LOAD, Technical Services, Plate Glass Division, Pittsburgh
Plate Glass, Pittsburgh, Pa.

Phillips, W., and Sheppard, D., 1982
PLANT CAST, PRECAST AND PRESTRESSED CONCRETE: A DESIGN GUIDE,
Prestressed Concrete Manufacturers Association of California

Portland Cement Association, 1980
PORTLAND CEMENT PLASTER (STUCCO) MANUAL, Portland Cement Association, Skokie, Ill.

Prestressed Concrete Institute, 1977
STRUCTURAL DESIGN OF ARCHITECTURAL PRECAST CONCRETE, MNL-121-77, Prestressed Concrete Institute, Chicago, Ill.

Prestressed Concrete Institute, 1982
GUIDE SPECIFICATION FOR GLASS FIBER REINFORCED CONCRETE PANELS, SPC-120-82, Prestressed Concrete Institute, Chicago, Ill.

Randall, F., et al., 1988
CONCRETE MASONRY HANDBOOK, Portland Cement Association, Skokie, Ill.

Reed, D. A., 1985
GLASS CLADDING DESIGN FOR TALL BUILDINGS, in *Proceedings of the NSF Indo–U.S. Workshop on Wind Disaster Mitigation,* Madras, India, December 16–20

Reed, D. A., 1986
CLADDING DESIGN FOR TALL BUILDINGS, in *Proceedings of the 3rd ASCE Engineering Mechanics Specialty Conference,* Los Angeles, Calif., April

Reed, D. A., 1987
AN EXPERT SYSTEM FOR GLASS CLADDING RISK ASSESSMENT, in *Proceedings of the Structural Engineering Congress '87,* Orlando, Fla., August

Reed, D. A., and Simiu, E., 1983
WIND LOADING AND STRENGTH OF CLADDING GLASS, U.S. Department of Commerce, National Bureau of Standards, Center for Building Technology, N.B.S. Building Science Series, 154, May

Ridout, G., 1989
LOSING ITS MARBLE, *Building,* vol. 254, no. 17, p. 61, April

Sabbagh, K., 1989
SKYSCRAPER, Macmillan in Association with Channel Four Television Company Limited, London

Sack, R., et al., 1981
SEISMIC RESPONSE OF PRECAST CURTAIN WALLS IN HIGHRISE BUILDINGS, Final Project Report, NSF Grant PFR-772000884, Moscow, Idaho

Sakamoto, I., et al., 1984
PROPOSALS FOR ASEISMIC DESIGN METHOD ON NONSTRUCTURAL ELEMENTS, in *Proceedings of the 8th World Conference on Earthquake Engineering,* San Francisco, Calif., July 21–28, vol. V, pp. 1093–1100

Schaupp, W., 1967
AUSSENWAND: BEKLEIDUNG, WÄRMEDÄMMUNG, FEUCHTIGKEITSSCHUTZ (EXTERNAL WALLS: CLADDING, THERMAL INSULATION, DAMP-PROOFING), translated by Irene and Harold Meek, Crosby Lockwood, London

Shand, E. B., 1985
GLASS ENGINEERING HANDBOOK, 2d ed., McGraw-Hill, New York

Shinkai, 1984
UNITED STATES–JAPAN JOINT TECHNICAL COORDINATING COMMITTEE INTERIM SUMMARY REPORT ON TESTS OF A SEVEN STORY REINFORCED CONCRETE BUILDING, *Journal of Structural Engineering,* vol. 110, no. 10, pp. 2392–2411, October

Simiu, E., and Lozier, D. W., 1975
THE BUFFETING OF TALL STRUCTURES BY STRONG WINDS, U.S. Department of Commerce, National Bureau of Standards, Center for Building Technology, NBS Building Science Series 74, October

Simiu, E., and Scanlon, R. H., 1978
WIND EFFECTS ON STRUCTURES, Wiley, New York, 1978

Simiu, E., Reed, D., et al., 1984
RING-ON-RING TEST AND LOAD CAPACITY OF CLADDING GLASS, U.S. Department of Commerce, National Bureau of Standards, Center for Building Technology, N.B.S. Building Science Series 162, August

Solomon, N. B., 1990
MADE IN JAPAN, *Architecture,* vol. 79, no. 8, August

Southern Building Code Congress International, 1979
STANDARD BUILDING CODE, Southern Building Code Congress International, Birmingham, Ala.

Sraeel, H., 1989
GLASS BUILDING FACADES: WHAT'S HOT, WHAT'S NOT, *Buildings,* vol. 83, no. 4, pp. 92–94, April

Stucco Manufacturers' Association, 1985
SPECIFICATIONS AND STANDARDS FOR MANUFACTURED STUCCO FINISHES, Stucco Manufacturers Association, Sherman Oaks, Calif.

Underwriters Laboratories, 1987
GLASS BLOCKS (120 IW7) HOHT, Underwriters Laboratories, Inc., Northbrook, Ill.

U.S.A.–Japan Research Seminar on Wind Effects on Structures Proceedings, 1976
WIND EFFECTS ON STRUCTURES: PROCEEDINGS OF THE SECOND U.S.A.–JAPAN RESEARCH SEMINAR ON WIND EFFECTS ON STRUCTURES, edited by Hatsuo Ishizaki and Arthur N. L. Chiu, University of Hawaii Press, Honolulu

Wang, M. L., 1986
U.S. SIDE FINAL REPORT: NONSTRUCTURAL ELEMENT TEST PHASE, U.S.–JAPAN COOPERATIVE RESEARCH PROJECT ON A FULL SCALE TEST FRAME, NSF Grant CEE 82-0812

Wang, M. L., 1987
CLADDING PERFORMANCE ON A FULL SCALE TEST FRAME, *Earthquake Spectra, The Professional Journal of the EERI,* vol. 3, no. 1, pp. 119–174, February

Williams, S., 1990
EXTERNAL CLADDING SYSTEM LAUNCHED, *Ceramic Industries International,* Official Journal of the British Pottery Managers Association, vol. 100, no. 1083, p. 11, October

Wilson, F., 1981
THE CHANGING NATURE OF BUILDING SKINS, *Architecture,* vol. 78, no. 3, pp. 66–71, March

Wright, G., 1991
WALL SYSTEMS STRIVE TO FOIL MOISTURE INTRUSION, *Building Design and Construction,* pp. 62–65, May

Zappa, A., 1989
LE COPERTURE METALLICHE, *Ville Giardini,* no. 234, pp. 38–46, February

Contributors

The following is a list of those who have contributed manuscripts for this Monograph. The names, affiliations, and countries of each author are given.

Bruce Bassler, Iowa State University, Ames, Iowa, USA
Lawrence Carbary, Dow Corning Corporation, Midland, Michigan, USA
Hal Iyengar, Skidmore, Owings & Merrill, Chicago, Illinois, USA
Jerome M. Klosowski, Dow Corning Corporation, Midland, Michigan, USA
Victor C. Mahler, Mahler Architectural Consultants, New York, New York, USA
Dorothy Reed, University of Washington, Seattle, Washington, USA
Isao Sakamoto, Faculty of Engineering, The University of Tokyo, Tokyo, Japan
Jerry G. Stockbridge, Wiss, Janney, Elstner Associates, Inc., Northbrook, Illinois, USA
Marcy Li Wang, Marcy Li Wang Architect, Berkeley, California, USA
Tomonair Yashiri, Building Research Institute, Ministry of Construction, Tsukuba, Japan
Gary Zwayer, Wiss, Janney, Elstner Associates, Inc., Northbrook, Illinois, USA

Name Index

The following list cites the page numbers on which the indicated names are mentioned. The list includes the authors as well as other individuals or organizations named in the text.

Names followed by years refer to bibliographic citations that are included in the appendix entitled "References/Bibliography."

Subject Index